Jesus

BOOK ONE

Channeled by Al Miner and Lama Sing

Jesus - Book 1

Copyright ©2007 by Al Miner

2nd Edition 2017

Cover art and book design by Susan M. Miner

ISBN 9780979126246
Library of Congress Control Number: 2007908614

1. Psychics 2. Trance Channels 3. Christ 4. Christ Spirit
I. Miner, Al II. Lama Sing III. Title

Printed in the United States of America

For other books and products, or to write Al Miner,
visit our website: www.lamasing.org

✝

Dedication

The collection of readings on Jesus would not be as complete or exhaustive as they are without the tireless dedication of my dear friends, Ken and Nancy of North Carolina.

For over thirty years they have sought to uncover missing information on Jesus, and to gain insights and understanding of His life and works. So I thank you, my dear friends, for helping me bring these works back, that they can be shared in the same loving spirit you held while seeking them.

Acknowledgment

I thank you, Stu, for the tireless contribution of your talent and beautiful spirit, and Diana, for your dedicated assistance.

Along the way, many individuals were involved in the process of bringing these works into print. From my heart, I thank you all.

—Al Miner

TABLE OF CONTENTS

Editor's Notes:

With the exception of a few words here and there, what you are about to read are the words of Lama Sing given in fourteen separate sessions (called readings), channeled by Al Miner. Questions that were sent in by the sponsor were read by Al at the opening, after which he placed himself into the trance state. Lama Sing would then enter the dimension of Earth, borrowing Al's voice for the reading.

Even though the name Lama Sing has been assigned to these readings, there is actually always a group involved. Depending upon the topic, sometimes the number is massive and sometimes it is a handful; sometimes they are speaking to a group and sometimes to an individual they know will one day get the message – in essence, speaking to one and all, as well as to only one and only all, curious, but true. Throughout the reading, they defer to one another just as we do when in a group discussion. This information may be of value as you read, so you don't stumble when they sometimes change, even in a single paragraph, from an archaic form of speech to a more modern one, or from the singular to the plural.

The name Channel is used by Lama Sing in place of Al, because to use the name Al would essentially serve to call him – call him from that consciousness to which he is taken that prevents his personal involvement and influence in what is given in the reading. There is only one known occasion in which Lama Sing used Al's given name. The reason given was that the depth of his channeled state was being tested.

Lastly…

There are places where Lama Sing emphasizes a thought by speaking the words quote/end-quote. To let the reader know that those emphases are Lama Sing's, as opposed to the transcriber's, the words quote/end-quote have been put in the text as well as the quotation marks themselves.

The word dis-ease is used by Lama Sing to mean, not only illness and such, but "first and foremost, a lack of ease in spirit, mind, and/or emotion, which are then precipitated into the physical body."

Lama Sing's use of words such as ye, thee, whom, and he is often contrary to conventional, but the meaning will be clear.

Father, we offer these questions to You in the form of a very humble prayer, in the hope that You would guide us to understand not only the aspects of the question, but all those things which You would know and see to be beneficial from this teaching from the Bible and that You would awaken within each of us such an understanding so as to further our progress and our joy in our search for Your presence. We ask this in the name of the Master, the Christ, and we thank You, Father. Amen. —Al Miner

Father, we ask that Thou would look upon us now as we seek to serve humbly in this work of some light, which is now before us. Help Thou us then, Father, to be that which is Thy holy instrument through which that information shall pass, as is according to Thy Will and purpose, and which ever bears honor to Thy Son, the Master, the Christ. That there shall be inspired within each who hear same, some memory of those times past wherein they, we, and the Master were as one with You. We pray as well on behalf of all those souls in all realms who are presently in some need and for whom none are in joyous prayer. In humble joy for this opportunity of service in Your name, we thank thee, Father. Amen. —Lama Sing

---

1 - *The Christmas Story*

LAMA SING COMMENTARY

There comes first the sound, which is that of glory in a form of singing, in a form of radiant music, which can be heard not with the ear but with the very soul and spirit of those who would heed same. For through the veil of darkness which envelops the Earth, there can be felt, and yea now seen, a light, growing, becoming more brilliant.

Even now as we view from the Earth plane, it can be perceived on the horizon in the distance. Fingers of various hues of light seem to leap forth and touch gently all other lights in the heaven, and we know this to be the soul which is about to enter the Earth... He who shall be called the Christ. As its brilliance grows, as closer it draws unto the Earth, there are others who perceive it now, moved from a strange but beautiful stirring from within their beings. Drawn unto awareness of their senses, their gaze moves quickly about them, that they might perceive what is taking place.

Our attention is now drawn unto these, who have come to be known as the kings, whose simultaneous recognition of this Light of the Christ wondrously draws them unto the same pathway. In the raiment of its growing brilliance, they excitedly and reverently discuss what it is they feel and sense, each having their own method, their own manner, of divination: one, from a source within, guided by an amulet; the other, by the casting of those things which bear the Spirit of God; and yet another, the third, by the forces sensed intuitively and spiritually from realms beyond the material. All agree, and continue their journey, as this wondrous orb of light seems to move, in a way, drawing them.

Though dark, the night is filled with light, and the earth beneath their feet seems to become resilient as though reaching up to meet their feet and giving them strength to go forward. They move on, until, from a hillside some distance away, they see before them down unto a gentle valley, and a small village of no great renown with several dwelling places.

As we move from these entities, we see that the light reaches out again in an even bolder ray or shaft, as though to penetrate through a certain structure and to illuminate all within same. We find here, the faithful have gathered both near and about, to protect, to guide, those of importance who have journeyed so far to kneel before Him.

Several small children are crouching, to peer through the loosely fastened boards of the wall. One, within, turns, sees them, and casts a gaze of warmth, a loving smile, towards them. There are the creatures whose silence and whose gentle repose is indicative of a position of honor given to Him who is now before them. Present, also, are those of the Essenes: those who will teach and guide, those who will counsel, and those who will be the protectorate, not only of Jesus, but also of those who shall care and tend to His growth and needs.

Interacting with those forces, which now merge with the forces of Earth, are many spiritual forces, and many souls not in body and yet visible, not of the Earth, yet upon it. And we find the Angelic Host and those who are the servants of our Father's Will, all about us. There is, at this moment, no sense of darkness nor temperature, as though the entire atmosphere is warmed by the presence of that shaft of light.

We witness the merging of the soul to the body, and it is as though the Child before us becomes that light, and for a moment they are as one. The vision of this Soul and its wisdom and its pending journey are such so as to move the deepest emotion in even the strongest of those present. The creatures all rise and the entities present all kneel, almost in unison. As we behold the Master in this small body, He beholds us, and there is a bond which shall remain throughout eternity.

There is the consciousness of all souls of this moment in

all realms, in all lands; there is the presence of awareness of each soul that exists in this moment of time and consciousness. In this place or that, one or another may, for a moment in time, deny Him or His presence; but none will fail to know this bond. Though they may explain it in different terms or through different practice, all are brethren unto the Christ.

We find as the moments pass, the light in the heavens seems to change from its more spherical form, and now seems to send out great shafts of light as though reaching to the north, to the south, to the east, and to the west, as though the very essence of this Soul seeks to embrace the entirety of the Earth.

The sounds of the spheres, the etheric sounds, are all about us now, and each entity is fair aglow with the wonder of its presence. Each entity present is illuminated from the soul. And the love which is in the glance of each entity is unmistakable, as one without remorse, judgment, fear, guilt, frustration, anger, bitterness. Only love and compassionate understanding seem to remain. It is as though this moment shall exist in time and space for all eternity.

There is the thought in the mind of one present, "How can it be that in this, so humble a place, such a mighty and wondrous Soul is come into the Earth?" It is as though His very Soul speaks into all our minds: I come to lead thee, not to rule thee. I come in this, the lowest, that I might show each of thee that all are equal; and neither a place, a substance, or a thing can long endure between us as an obstacle.

We find, even further here, in the hills, many of the shepherds are bowed in silent prayer. The animals all face towards the star. None are grazing. All are gazing wistfully, with the reflection of this star's brilliance in their eyes, returning as a sea of brilliant lights in the reflection of their eyes and very spirits. And all of the flowers afield begin to bloom in the darkness, lending their perfume to the night air.

It begins softly at first... the calling of the dove, and then the others, and others, begin their songs, seemingly to sing with the Angelic Hosts the proclamation of His presence. Night and day have merged into one. It is as though all souls have disrobed of their body and that which is self, to show for this moment in time that they are bound together in a sense of unison, which must emerge in that finality of experience towards that which is the latter time of eternity.

They come, first appearing as a descending cloud moving from the heavens, first one, then another, and then great multitudes, as they descend from their spheres and the ray of light from His soul-consciousness, to pay homage and express their dedication and love for His task and His presence. All of the prophets who have gone before, visible only to those who can see with the spirit, lay before Him, each one, a certain thing. One brings a gift of unending patience. Another brings the gift of forgiveness. Another brings compassion. Another, love. Another brings faith. And charity. And on it goes for time untold in length, they descend and gather and place the most precious gifts that they have to give before Him.

There is the movement in the heavens as the alignment of those spheres once again reaches conjunction. A great rent in all the spheres comes together with a surge of energy, not that which is displeasing, but as though one feels a flow of undulating warmth over their being. And it is known now that it is complete. The unison of His consciousness with this body, and the awareness of the Christ within, is complete.

THE SPIRIT OF THE CHRIST WITHIN

What, then, shall ye bear in your present life? The knowledge of this story, told and retold in this way and that, emphasizing this aspect or that? What, then, shall ye hold?

Each Christ-mass, hold that thought that at the instant of unification of body, mind, and spirit unto this, the man called Jesus, there was fashioned within each of you this same seed. Then when you next celebrate His mass, celebrate that mass within, and try each day of Earth consciousness to nourish it just a bit.

Give it, then, thy gifts of love, of faith, of charity, forgiveness, compassion, all of those aspects as ye know are His. As ye do, know ever that thou art one step closer unto that moment when the very finger of God shall pierce through the darkness of those realms of Earth to light upon thee, to proclaim to all that: this is My child, of whom I am most pleased.

In that which is the spirit of the Christ, we here, who are most humble to be with thee, proclaim to you that this is what shall be:

Each of you shall have your moment as the Christ. Each of you shall be born into that of the simplicity of the Earth, shall be raised up under the care and guidance of loving souls, and shall use each of those gifts given by loving entities in these realms, whereupon, there shall emerge the jewel of your soul, which is the promise of God unto thee: the Christ.

And in that moment where there must be the decision to cling to the flesh or to cleave from it that jewel, ye shall know the answer to all that ye seek. And there shall be remembered, then, not only this mass, but that moment when you were united with the Christ.

2 - The Childhood of Jesus

CHANNEL/AL MINER: From Biblical accounts we know almost nothing about Jesus as a boy. Please give a narrative description of what you consider the important aspects of the childhood of Jesus.

SPONSOR'S QUESTIONS

1. When Jesus was a little boy, what was His personality like? Was He a perfect being who sat around being "holy" all the time? Or was He a normal child who talked back to His parents, got in fights with other kids in the neighborhood, and played in the dirt? Was He a sweet child or a boisterous child? Was He an introvert or an extrovert?

2. As a child, was the veil very thin for Him? Could He communicate consciously with His guides and God? Or did He temporarily "forget" as children seem to do and have to re-learn this?

3. Did He live in what we would call a nuclear family or in a communal environment like a kibbutz? Were all the people around Him Essenes? Or was there a mixture of people of differing beliefs around Him?

4. Did He go to school with other children? Who were His childhood friends? Did some of them later become His Disciples or followers? What was His relationship to His cousin John?

5. Later in childhood, did His parents sometimes forget His spiritual stature? Did they know His mission? Did He know His mission, or did He have to discover it?

6. When He became a teenager was He interested in girls? Did He find them attractive? Did He ever have a sweetheart? Did He have the usual sexual desires of an adolescent male? Or

was He always about His Father's work?

7. What role did Joseph play? What was their relationship like? Did Joseph teach his son carpentry? Did he teach Jesus about spiritual subjects? What happened to Joseph in the latter years of Jesus' life?

8. We assume that Mary played the role of a traditional mother. But what other role did She play in Jesus' life? What was His relationship with Her? What did He learn from Her?

Please include any other information that you think we might find interesting or useful.

LAMA SING COMMENTARY

We shall at the onset of this work make certain changes here in order that we can preserve, as it were, certain qualities and characteristics as are a part of this work in the ongoing nature of service through this soul, this Channel; that such as might be imparted here and shortly hereafter may flow according to the Father's Will, and not bring about that change which may in any sense be inappropriate or less than timely for the Channel or any others involved in same.

Therefore, we seek from the grouping as called the Elders or the Brotherhood, who are ever a part of the Master's own light, those references as we are permitted to offer here in response to the inquiry now before us.

In order, then, of the inquiries before us, and with a certain degree of addendum here and there, we proceed.

THE EARLY YEARS

It should be understood here that no small preparation was made prior to the entry of the Master, the Christ. Therefore, there was, as to be expected from such a preparation, considerable presence, both in terms of the peoples, the entities (that is to say, non-physical), and those forces and activities as are a part of the preparation which went before. These were ever-present as an influence, as a guiding force, as a protective mechanism of sorts, through which and by which means there might be perpetuated the awakening, the growth, the nurturing, the preparation, and all that sort which was to follow.

What He Was Like

The personality was basically light, not flippant but casual, joyful, eager in the anticipation of each new discovery. Often augmented by the enthusiastic and positive attitudes of those who were aplenty about Him: the Essenes and others who came from near and far to be a part of these works and to contribute according to their individual destinies those things which they would to this as a collective work and a thought-form, which was and is the standard by which all shall evermore be measured: the Christ.

The measure of perfection, being somewhat subjective and according to the time therein, could be considered a good lad, although not in the sense that one would consider (quote) "without error" (end quote), this is to say that the process of experimentation, the process of being in the carnal (that is, in the Earth) and being a part of same through the acceptance of this as a physical vehicle or body. So there was, then, to the degree that one would measure same, a certain bit of spontaneity and jubilance, as is natural for the progression of a child.

There was a considerable degree of what we would call preservation of the intactness of the thought-form that was builded and foreseen and prophesied. So this was like a shelter of sorts, in the sense that no real harm could be brought to bear against the Master, but there were sufficient experiences prevailing so as to allow for the development and the understanding of those things which challenge humankind, and those who are incarnated virtually in all realms. Thus, again, there were the lessons, as it were, brought about so wisely by experience and by shared experiences between Himself, His cousin John, and others to be sure.

We do not find that He spoke back to His parents, in the sense that we comprehend that term. For there was an attitude of respect that was a mainstay of all of these teachings, be they those brought from the Eastern or those from the present or those which are mid-way between same. So, this was not a thought nor was it, in that sense, a testing of a child against authority. There was the continual spirit of wellbeing and joyfulness maintained on the inner circle, or within the confines of the consciousness, preserved primarily by the Essenes.

Joyful Childhood

There were those occasions when wrestling was a part of the activity, but not for the besting of one another but for the strengthening, as was the tradition among the Essenes: physical strength in the form of endurance and prowess, not in terms of the boisterous brute strength, but the capacity to endure, to sustain, and to prolong life in dire circumstances. These things were a part of the physical activity. Running, jumping and such, seemingly as marathons, day after day, were much to the delight of the Master and those of His associates, oft times to the fatigue of some of the elderly Essenes assigned for the preservation, the guardianship (with a note of loving humor). Not boisterous, but strong. Convicted in what He believed, and this continually growing. Not necessarily excessive in His sweetness, just balanced. See?

Similarly, in terms of His openness or reservation, reasonably balanced. Tending later to be a bit more introverted, and then after that more extroverted. But always, in the later stages, in great control, guided by the inner Spirit, the Light from the Father Himself.

The child Jesus was conscious, in the sense of being aware, that He and the Father are as One. But we should add here that most, if not all, children have this consciousness. It becomes a question of definition and reference to determine whether or not the veil was thin or normal, in that sense. So we would have to state in the spirit of your question, that it was normal in the early childhood, but then, a thin veil is normal for children (referring to ages one through about five to six, possibly seven, years).

There was no need, essentially, for Him to communicate consciously or in the direct sense with guides and with God, although this did occur on numerous occasions, and often in the dreams. He delighted in pressing his father, Joseph, and the others who were of the Essenial Council and Protectorate, "What does this or that mean?"

There was often jest and humor, largely pouring from Him, causing those who were His counsel to re-think their answers very carefully and to oft times expand upon them to the degree that they became weary. (Much humor here.)

We cannot state that He forgot, in the sense of your question, for He didn't truly remember in the first place (using the same perspective and terminology as you are implying in your question). It is, rather, that He was, as planned, normal; and afforded a normal, though very secure, environment in which to evolve, that is, to grow the physical.

It was recognized by the Essenes and by the others who were of varying philosophical positioning (that being both philosophical and theosophical, to be sure) that here there must be some proper foundational evolution, in order that the harmony that was to be so necessary in later stages could be well laid out. It is difficult for one who has not ever been immersed in water to teach others how to swim. The consciousness was appropriate for this as a work, as a part of the development. And as such, there was given the normal preservation and, you could call it "cloak of immunity" (put that in quotes, please) that enables the youthful consciousness and knowledge of an entity just having entered the Earth from being too tainted, too burdened, too limited, by the existing thought-forms of others whose longevity in Earth far exceed this as the youthful entity. Therefore, this [childhood] was given a sort of spiritual cloak; and, in the literal sense, a cloak indicative of certain levels of remarkable authority of office, but symbolic only to the inner circle of the Essenes. And this was always present, as were those who were a part of the Essenes, including Judy, Josie and, to be sure, Editha at the early days (and many others, see), those in the responsibility for the nurturing, the care, the overseeing and such.

OTHERS INVOLVED

Regarding your question of a family, in terms of nuclear versus the communal, both would have to apply. Although one would, observing from the outer, have to comment, we would suppose, that this certainly was a communal environment, judging from all the entities near and some distance away. Yet, the cohesiveness and oneness of the integral family unit was ever-present, strong. There was no shortcoming of oneness nor love, which was the continual outpouring, not only to the Master, Jesus, but to the others: His comrades, including, of course, John.

Essene Community

Then there were those in the later years who came to inspire, to acquaint, to bring the precursive stimulative experiences as would relate to joyful song, to dance, to music, to color, to the astrological, to all sorts of methods of divination and sight that were a part of the teachings of the School of Prophets, and those works which became later woven all throughout the Essenian Council's teachings, their law, their tenets, and their works. But do not misinterpret that the Essenes were a largely localized grouping of just one descendency or nature, but a very broad and diverse collection of wonderful different tones of expression, understanding, and belief. For essentially, all those who felt called were welcomed by the Essenes. And for the most part, so long as the tenets of the Essenial law or teaching were preserved and upheld, they were accepted.

The outreach was great, although this was not the primary intent but, rather, that of the preparation. Certain of this grouping considered the preparation to include the outreach and the establishment of other, as could be called, satellites or encampments or other small groupings along the way. For the seers, the prophets – not only Anna, but the others, as well – well looked upon these potentials and knew them. According to the internal mechanisms, each was free to choose to follow that work and that pathway as they felt inwardly guided to do. Yet, there were those in the inner circle, as it might be called, who were doggedly determined to hold a core nucleus or nuclei that would be the shelter, that would be the protectorate, and that would make the way passable and overcome any obstacle, any limitation, to preserve and make the way passable for what they foresaw: the Light of man.

So the mixture, as such, was from diverse followings, teachings, and beliefs all the way from the Far Eastern to the Near, the Persians, the Indians, and others all along the way. And there were the Greeks, and even the Romans, involved here. And many, of course, who were of the strictest heritage of the inner Jewish faith and teachings, even priests. For was not John's father one such? And did not his zealousness cause him to lose his own life?

The Inner Circle

The inner circle was primarily Essene and their training was profound. They were, first, skilled in the School of the Prophets, resurrected or re-illuminated by the Essenes one hundred years previously, as was established earlier by Elijah, and perpetuated down through the lesser prophets, through Samuel and others. While this seemed to dim for a time, the truth and the tenets and such were always maintained. They were intentionally not quite visible to those who were on the outside, but perfect and pure to those who pledged their life, their existence, their lifetime, to carry the truth to the next, and that one to the next, and that one after that to the next, and so forth. So, between three/perhaps three-hundred-twenty Earth years until it flowered again here for all of the Earth to behold.

It brought forth the issuance of those who knew them-selves to be among the potential, those from whom there would be (quote) "chosen" (end quote) the vehicle by which the Master might enter. This one, then, became, of course, as is known, Mary. At Her side and as that one who would bear the words which would precede the Master, Elizabeth, and then of course her issue, John.

If you would think of a line of communication that was largely by word but occasionally otherwise, issuing forth, carried by those who were emissaries somewhat involved in the commercial, somewhat involved in the communication, but always seeking to look for those signs, those signets, that would indicate this is the way, this is the choice, this is the opening through which He shall pass.

Yes, went to school with other children, though the schooling was not of the normal sense as you interpret same in the present. But it could be stated that it was viewed that His entire life was, as such, a (quote) "school" (end quote) wherein, in the latter days, He became the teacher.

The teachings, then, primarily those as were foreseen and decided by Judy, taught by Judy and some by Sophie. Josie was in the care of the body, the protection and preservation of the good health, the knowledge of the herbs, the foods, and such, which John took greatly to heart, for it was his way to be avid in this regard and to seek out certain degrees of independence, believing that the law of the Essenes was as his own life; the Master differing in this sense: that it was the spirit He felt of the Essenial law, which was to prepare Him foundationally but that the greater Spirit and Law was within.

There was somewhat of the sheltering from certain activities and entities; and the seers were constantly at hand to preserve, to protect, and to instruct the guard or guardians to move in this direction or that, to intercede here or there. While this was not (quote) "necessary" (end quote) – for the mantle of God's cloak was upon Him – it was, nonetheless, a part of the life's work, purposes, teachings, the works of numerous lifetimes cascaded into a collage of opportunity here. And it was the Master's spiritual choice to allow these entities to manifest so as they would, and so as would make that mark, His mark, upon the very signet of each soul who participated in any way in His works and in the preparation and making passable the way.

Childhood Playmates

It could be stated that anyone He met, He considered a friend. He did not have the consciousness to perceive entities as enemies; therefore, it is a moot point to call this one or that anything less than a friend. While there were others who came and went, and some teaching as to the ciphering and to the languages and such, occasionally others of the Essenes who were children given or dedicated unto the Essenian community were among His playmates and associates. Though there were not necessarily those we would single out here, for all were worthy and all were of significance, many of these (according to the intent of your question) were to become those the Master sent forth two by two to teach and do works in His name.

These – the childhood playmates, who were some number in their presence – were later, many of them, if not most of them, to be a part of the Master's works in one way or another.

Most of the childhood friends were of the Essenes and their associates, to be sure, for there were some Essenes who were recognized gladly for their spiritual wisdom and their insight in their own unique way. Some of these bore several wives and numerous children, and these were exposed to the Master and vice-versa for the goodness and broadening of His understanding, His outreach, and to prepare for the later days.

Each of these was blessed, as well, and many of these later became bearers of light in their own right, traveling to the distant corners of the Earth, not only (in that incarnation) in later years, but as the opening of the way for their spirit to bring light later in their own teaching and among diverse peoples.

The Essenes were not limited to the *then and now*, but among them were great seers, great prophets, great healers, entities of wondrous wisdom. And the association with the Essenes was broad and diverse and, thus, this spawned the best of all. See? No truth was sheltered or blocked for fear of it disrupting just the inner circle's certain dictum, but truth was considered truth, and if it manifested in this form or that, it was considered worthy and, as such, some portion of same was offered or presented. But the emphasis was not upon a thing, as such, but as a way of life... the nurturing of the environment, which would allow for the natural evolution and development of the physical, the mental, and the emotional.

So, yes, some of them later became His followers and/or Disciples and co-workers in the Light (which, incidentally, yet burns as a light) just as during those times of need, so shall the flame be kindled and brightened, and the true teachings come forth again. See?

His Cousin, John

The relationship with His cousin, John, was as expected, just so as Mary and Elizabeth, and such. But remember, Mary and Elizabeth were long-time followers of the Essenian law: given in childhood in the manner of speaking as being dedicated; not abandoned, not cast off, but given in the sense of a promise, an opportunity. This did not mandate that they would be this or that because they were given. Each step of the way had to be earned, had to be demonstrated in terms of the worthiness. The proof was in the expression, in the life.

In some respects, Jesus and John were significantly different in their childhood, until they were parted for a time. But there was the good camaraderie, the fondness for song and dance.

Joseph

They were often seen guided by Joseph, who loved the Hebraic hymns and psalms; and for many, many twilight and evening hours Joseph would be scolded for keeping the children up so late, violating the tenets and teachings of the Essene law. To which Joseph oft times replied, "The spirit is awake, why not the body?" (In other words, "They will endure.")

While there was little mention of the authority of Joseph, he was looked upon by those of the Essene community with great reverence. Therefore, few, if any, would approach him, save Judy, Ruth, Sophie, and Anna, who would be hard-pressed to be silent if they were of any mind that something was amiss. But even here, Joseph had the warmth and mellowness of one who was skilled of hand and light of heart in many respects. Though his age would seem to deny this, it would nonetheless come forth when the twilight time came. And after the tradition and after the purification and after the sacrifice and the rituals and such, which were aplenty among the Essenes (and, of course, among the Jewish law), here Joseph would bring forth the human side of these qualities, and in the somewhat forthright earthy nature as would be anticipated from one who worked with their hands as a carpenter or whatnot, his hands could clap out a tune.

There were ample, if not aplenty, musicians and singers among the inner grouping, the Essenes and such, and so, oft times there would be wondrous gatherings of song and song-festing and circles within circles, dancing rhythmically, to the delight of both John and Jesus, and the others to be sure.

HIS MISSION

It would be seemingly difficult, if at all possible, for the parents to (quote) "sometimes forget his spiritual purpose or stature" (end quote). For think of this: imagine yourselves being in the presence of such a wondrous grouping, illuminated entities, brilliant entities of great wealth and power secretly present, all seeking to be a part of the evolution of the Light of Mankind. Forget? Hardly. Except Joseph. He could pass off these things from time to time and burst into joyful song or point out the more humorous side of something intended to be, just so, serious.

We are aware of the knowledge you possess, and intent behind your questions: to bring forth information here in this gathering that will be moreso complete. With that as an acknowledgement that we recognize one another's position and purpose here (with a note of loving humor), we will proceed to offer information in response to your questions, albeit in your heart and mind the answers are clearly known.

His Parents' Awareness

Did they know of His mission? Certainly. They were Essenes. Mary, of course, being from early on dedicated to a way of life which followed utterly the Essene tradition and the law, literally; Elizabeth, as well, but Mary in the sense that She was identified at an early age as of one of those that would be selected from, in terms of that one who would bear the Light of God, who would be with the Child who shall become thereafter the Light unto the Earth. So certainly, here, from early age – four, five Earth years – Mary was knowledgeable of something of this sort, but ever joyful. For the tradition and heritage was to be joyful in all things, and the greater the sacrifice, the greater the opportunity for joy. That was the teaching, and it was met with enthusiasm.

For, consider the outer life, the other attitudes, the other activities then taking place in the Earth all about them. In a manner of speaking, they were of little difference than events in the Earth about you at this time. In fact, one could surmise from this that there is a direct parallel between that time – the preparation and the opening of the way – to the current time in your Earth. Which is the preparation? And who can say what shall follow and when?

Joseph

So, there was the knowledge, yes. And even though Joseph was not so much so on the inner circle for such a complete aspect of his life, his involvement was nonetheless dedicated. But when he was chosen, there was disbelief and some considerable time needed for him to balance with this. He was less aware than was Mary, who was and is, of course, the point of balance for the Master himself... then, in past, and always.

Jesus Himself

It cannot be answered just so that He did or did not know His mission, and that He did or did not have to discover it. For it is like holding a container of water, and asking one's self, "Do you think that this container of water knows that it is water?" Here again, the point is not necessary to be expressed, for whether it knows it is or not, it is water.

Therefore, whether or not the Child Jesus knew that He was and is the Christ is actually of no consequence, for He was and is the Christ. It is likened, again here, unto one looking into a mirror and asking of the mirror, "Who is it that looks back at me?" No matter what answer might come to one in mind or heart, it will always be a reflection of self, will it not? That self reflected is the physical; that self which is considered or which is pondered is the spiritual. So the childhood was the reflection of the potential within, but always the image of that which was to become recognized by all as the Christ.

TEEN YEARS

Was Always About His Father's Work

There was always a love for and a zest for life, and in the exuberance of those of His colleagues, anyone who would play a game. Not a game of winners and losers, but a game of strengthening and discovering, as was the Essenian teachings. They were not all pious. They had their ways of expressing joy. But invariably each of those (quote) "pleasures" (end quote) had an underlying purpose or meaning. (Good logistics, see.) Approaching the (as you call it) teenage years, He was about His Father's work, the beginning. The teaching became more thorough, and the opportunity for Him to bless those who came from distant lands and such as this as the exchange between both, this was fast under way at about the twelfth year.

The question regarding girls has no relevance, in the sense that one might look upon this as a light which has been turned on to full force, and ask, "Is there any darkness here?" It cannot endure in the light. Did the Master love? Deeply, fondly, and with a passion. Did He love girls because they were girls? No, He loved them for what He saw and felt in and from them. The Master was surrounded by women all throughout His early years. Up to approximately His twelfth or thirteenth year, you could consider that the majority of those about Him caring for Him, teaching Him, counseling, guiding and so forth, were female.

Certainly there were those (not the least of which, Joseph) who were present to provide some masculine counterpoint, as it were. But remember here, as well, the Master was in male body, and with the power and presence within Him – even with Mary there to guide, to love, to nurture and balance – a great number of feminine entities were considered by the Essenes to be almost mandatory to keep this light from bursting forth and to provide the counterpoint to His nature, His spirit. This contributed so much in later years to the remarkable balance, the remarkable ease, and the compassion with which He dealt with all manner of challenge. It was this that tempered, more than anything else, the human side, the emotion and such.

Delighted in Life

In many respects, John brought to light the dynamics of the feminine and the potential and the need for righteousness. He didn't do so essentially alone as John, but in the earlier time as Elias, the prophet, the originator (most state) of the School of the Prophets (though, to be sure, this was at hand for much of time in this form or another).

He found beauty in all things (so did the Master) and was able to look within to see the beauty.

He loved sleight-of-hand tricks, and those who were skilled in this sleight of hand, He would often question them, study them, until He perceived just how the mechanism was accomplished. The greater was the challenge, the more zealous was He to pursue same. John, on the other hand, often sat a step or two distant, studying pensively the purpose behind this, coming to the conclusion that this was yet another way to mask Truth, for his teaching was deep and broad according to the inner Essene law. Though he did not make light of this, he was often the source of amusement of both Jesus and a number of others, which he bore good-naturedly, as he knew himself as he was taught to know himself. He also knew the Master.

We have no references here to what you call sexual desires, for the Master was complete in the presence of Mary.

Mary and the Master have always been in perfect harmony, and where one is, the other is to be found, in this form or that. And so it is that in the light of this utterly perfect balance, which begins in the spirit and manifests in the flesh, such things as the creative desires (as are symbolized so often in the Earth in the sexual) had no similar meaning here. Indeed, the Essenes themselves taught, as a mainstay of their belief, piety, chastity, and all good qualities, which would not weaken under duress or stress or temptation. The Master's capacity to resist temptation at every turn, which would take him off to a path differing from that prophesied, was without weakness, was without failure.

There are no instances given here of any such sexual activities, nor the desire in the carnal. Remember this: He loved deeply, and He saw beauty often and admired same in the feminine. But He also saw beauty in the masculine and admired this, as well.

There was a uniqueness in the feminine which the Master deeply revered or held warmly. We should call this perhaps better than revered, but the completeness of the statement is ineffective without that term, hence it was given. The feminine, as the Master knew it to be and was embraced by the Essenes in this time, was looked upon as the utter receptiveness, that which could and did yield itself utterly unto the guidance and Spirit of God.

Therefore it was held very special in the inner circle, not to the diminishment of the masculine but actually uplifting aspects of the masculine. For the Essenian communities relied very heavily upon the feminine and, as such, this freed the masculine to do other works and to do and accomplish other activities which were according to the tenets of those times, which had little, if any, reflection of honor or such for the feminine, except those high-born.

So it was that the masculine were often those who went forth and accomplished those interactive works as were mandated by the dictums of those times or the theosophy or the law, you see. For which one who transgressed against same could actually be put to death or imprisoned forevermore. So this was no small matter, do you see, but one of significance. The Master, seeing this to be the freeing of the receptive – the potential for hope for the future, as those who would bear forth new life – yes, He saw beauty in this. He saw the creative spirit of God, His Father, our Father, as this could be expressed only in the form of the feminine, no matter how much the masculine expression might attempt to emulate same.

The balance between the male-female could not have been much better, we should think, than it was here in these times, for there was no competitiveness in the sense of one trying to lure the other under their control. Mark you well, there was no lack of authority here, for once an office was given, the authority represented by that office was taken very much so to heart, to spirit, to mind. That entity then bore that responsibility in their every waking moment, and in quite a few of those moments wherein they were aslumber (humorously given, see).

So, while it was not necessarily so that He was (quote) "always about His Father's works" (end quote), He was always guided by the strength of spirit which was His life. Picture, then, an environment in which such competitive aspects as are generally alluded to in sexual connotation were non-existent, where male and female were honored equally; not one for this and one for that, but equally. He saw and was exposed to the migration of entities from this role to that, that anyone who was at hand when a certain need arose would fill it quickly and with honor for the opportunity, be that to cook a meal, to sing a song, or to mend a bit of clothing.

Delightful Times

The male entities often were those who made the procurements, who guarded the teachings, the scrolls, the writings. Very often they were called upon to recount same to the Master, to John, and to the others, with some such as Judy or Sophie or any one of the others, including Mary and, often, Joseph, to expound or to amplify a point or two.

Then there would come quite naturally, as was the custom then as now, the sort of free-for-all discussion which Jesus took particular delight in, as did John, as did many of the others, as each entity presented point and counterpoint viewpoints of what had been read or taught or sung or demonstrated.

There were often opportunities wherein certain of the entities would act. In other words, there would be a bit of a sonnet or play or drama just to alter the mood or the tenor. This would be with complete accompaniment, musical and whatnot. The entire collection would gather and they would all be radiating joyful anticipation. They would stomp and clap when appropriate, and weep and wail aloud with good-natured mock sadness, as simple things, as right and wrong and good and (quote) "evil" (end quote), so as to say that which grows and that which does not, and all these things were depicted

Think not, then, this as a dreary, morose time. Rather, think of this as a time filled with joy, and lots of activities. Hardly a moment here or there where someone wasn't at hand to bring a fresh fruit, or a new song, or a riddle, which was to John's particular delight, and to the Master's amusement, for He always saw the answer a step or two before John.

Sorrows

Then there were those times wherein they were shown the masses. Here, there were expeditionary forces, so to say, preceded by certain groups of Essenes, flanked by groups of Essenes, and followed by groups of Essenes, so as not to interfere at such close quarters with the thought-form that the Master and others with Him were seeking to discover. And so the Master saw limitation. He saw dis-ease and pestilence, and He sorrowed over this. He saw those of wealth and of stature, and it angered Him. He saw those who had much and those who had nothing. He saw those of health and self-aggrandizement, and those whose bodies, minds, and even their souls were heavy-burdened.

These times were followed by times of purification, thankfulness, and celebrations of prayerful thanksgiving, which included feasts. And the Master always asked that those things not needed would be sent and given to those whom He had observed who had naught. This was done with utter dispatch, and each one, the Master could identify by this or that, often amplified by John adding, "Yes, and they had on that tunic..." or "...that sash." They were of one mind in this regard and sought to bring ease to those in need. There were others here, other children, as well. So, in a manner of speaking, even though not the primary intent or thought-form, it could be said that He was (quote) "always about His Father's works" (end quote), though not in the traditional or formal sense as the question implies.

THE INFLUENCE OF JOSEPH AND MARY

We have given considerable, here, regarding Joseph. It is somewhat to the discredit of Joseph that so little is given elsewhere. He was utterly of strength, like a stout beam that would support the mid-members of an abode. And because of the immensity of the weight often placed upon these beams, Joseph's significance comes to the forefront from such a perspective, for as story upon story was added to same, the greater was the responsibility of the main members at the bottom floor, this was Joseph.

Upon the upper echelons of this imaginary dwelling you would find other entities – aspects of the Essenes, and Eastern, and others – who sought to fulfill a sort of collage that would be imagined in the house of life into which the Master entered. So it was, then, that Joseph was strong, though not verbally; firm and foundationally rock-like, though he let others demonstrate this.

The Relationship: Joseph, and Jesus and John

The relationship between Joseph, and Jesus and John, and many of the other children, was one to bring a smile to the heart of the most staunch and serious and dedicated purveyor of wisdom that the Essenian inner chamber had to offer. Not one would withstand seeing the man Joseph upon his fours, all fours, with Jesus as a small lad, John, and sometimes two others on his mighty back as he sought to emulate some beast of burden, accompanying his actions with very bold verbal outcries of their nature.

To see this one who was respected and upheld with some reverence, as we stated, by many of the Essenes equating himself to the level of a child and being a child, was a shining example for others who tended to become a bit too stiff in their stature, taking a bit too much seriousness in their office and duties.

Ofttimes, Joseph would gradually be accompanied by two, three, and others of the Essene uprightness (we could call it), frolicking about in the dust and dirt. They were not above such, but Joseph was no small example or inspiration to them. It was a time of delight for the Master, and equally so for Joseph. It is written here among certain of the Essene records that it was this willingness of heart for which Joseph was chosen, and it was this complete dedication to the joy and good health of the Master's childhood that Joseph was blessed to have future children. But there is no certainty in this, for it is the observation of those who were present. From here [those gathered in this group who are presenting this information], we would [agree with this Essene record, and] state he was well blessed, and worthy of that blessing.

We couldn't state here, with the kind of commentary and enthusiasm, that Joseph was, as such, a teacher of spiritual matters to Jesus. But then, when is the spirit gladdened? When at study? Or when it is experiencing the wonders, the beauties, the marvels, to be found in sharing joyful times? We should think the latter is the more self-evident. While the other, the spiritual study, may give the teaching and the intellectual, that which is found in the involvement (the one to one, or one to ten, as was often the case here) this would be the joy.

Did he teach spiritual subjects? Yes, he taught how to have a zest, a love for life. He found marvel in each creature, great and small, and he shared this with the Master, and ofttimes many others of childhood tenure, and was looked upon with great favor by those. In the literal meaning, it could be said that he taught spiritual subjects by living them and by being an example of one facet of spiritual teaching.

This love, this oneness with the Earth and with life and with nature, with song, with colors, with all of existence, was an inspiration evermore to the Master in all of His works which were to follow and that which literally sustained John... in other words, enabled him to live in any part of the land, no matter how arid or how wild it might be. He knew how, thanks to Joseph and certain others, to survive. It could be said that John's joy from the forces of nature were among the highest, and this was a gift to him from Joseph.

Joseph's Departure

In the latter years, Joseph departed. The Master was called to return to His homeland from the East, and gave much reverence and many blessings to this good soul who had once again accompanied Him and Mary in this experience. And so there is gladness all throughout the Kingdoms of Light for the presence of Joseph.

Mary's Role

It is difficult to put into thought-forms, much less words through this Channel, what you would call the role of Mary to or with Jesus. It is like stating to you that the Earth has two polar influences (in the magnetic sense), a north and a south. And so it is that we might consider here similarly for Jesus and Mary important roles such as this. Their life together in this and in past incarnations, and in the present and future works, is like the perfect alignment of two polar influences, between and upon which all of existence can find balance. And so they are, in this sense, as the example: the Light, the Teaching, the Way.

As Mother, Teacher, and Underpinning

Here ever as the good Essene, raised in that tradition, taught how to understand nature, to know the good plants, the good foods, the good talismans, the good influences, both in terms of the esoteric and the literal. The guidance was to teach the Master gradually how to use His dreams, His insights, His visions; and to be a strength to the Master in times of sadness, which were aplenty, as would be the normal for a child; and then, ever, to be the underpinning, the support, the contributor to that flow of energy, which was and is His Light. So as the flame needs its fuel, so was Mary to the Master. Not consumed, but by the bringing together, the production of that called Light.

It is inestimable to recount here Her contributions to the Master. They are as a multitude. They are as the celestial bodies in your evening sky. And to call this one brighter or more beautiful than the next is only due to one's perspective, one's viewpoint, and one's interest or individuality. But in the utterness of humility, we offer this in response to the spirit of your question... Of all those in the Earth, as a child the Master loved Mary. He loved Her without reservation, and still does. He saw in Her not just His mother but found in Her a sense of completeness, the counterpoint to a musical progression, the harmonic that makes the richness of any tone, the complementary color that makes one so radiant, and on and on.

She gave and was supportive to all of the other teachings. Always present but never seeking for Herself; there to comfort, to hold secure, and to give warmth – loving, human, physical warmth – to Her child. She was aided greatly, in the needs of the Master and the entire family, by those of the inner Essene circle assigned and chosen to be one with them.

The teaching, the work, was to continually and gradually inspire the Master to look within. The dreams were matched to outer symbols. And the Master awakened, step-by-step, grain-by-grain, until that time was reached when Mary knew that She must now draw herself into the foundational aspects of the Master's work, and so She did. But ever guided and supported, cared for, by the Essenes, and always unto Her own work, dedicated. See?

Joy Beyond the Tearful End

She was not idle when the Master was about His minis-try, but ever active. Counsel was sought from Her, not unlike as counsel was sought from the Master; but those who sought from Mary and those with Her were a part of the outreach.

As the Master's works unfolded according to the prophe-cies, She was there before Him, before the works, preparing, guiding, instructing, and counseling. This did not minimize the authority of the others nor their offices, for they did not com-pete in this regard but looked to the one work, which they knew unto the tearful end. And yet, they knew beyond this to the joy of coming together upon their individual completion of their sojourn in the Earth. The Children of God are within His Light, ever. So was the Master, and so are each of you.

What the Master learned from Mary was a reflection of His own nature, seasoned surely with the loving compassion as is Her counterpart to Him, and His to Her. So they bring light where there is darkness. But there is no darkness in your hearts, for you are children of God.

CLOSING COMMENTS

It is for each of you that the Master's works were so dedi-catedly prepared for. Centuries took place in their normal unfolding, and the truth was guarded, held secure, utterly.

Lives were dedicated, by the score upon score, utterly obscure to the knowledge of the Earth, but known here among us, and among the Father's many Kingdoms of Light.

And so, as you look upon that as we have given it above, it is our humble prayer that you will find something that will inspire you. We are also cognizant of many good works which have gone before; it has been our intent not to duplicate where unnecessary those works, but to augment, to contribute to, the same events from just another perspective.

As you would gather twelve about a certain series of events and after a time question them individually about what import they observed, you would probably note twelve distinct emphases upon twelve individual events or portions thereof.

So the point is, in your heart there is Truth: The Master walked upon the Earth as the man called Jesus to offer you the Light with which to find that Truth.

3 - The Education of Jesus

CHANNEL/AL MINER: From Biblical accounts, as with the childhood of Jesus, we know nothing about the education of Jesus. Please give a narrative description of the important aspects of the education and training of Jesus.

SPONSOR'S QUESTIONS

1. Who were the main teachers of Jesus, and what was their training? How were they chosen? Would you please tell us something about them? Were there others besides the Essenes who trained Him?

2. What were the main lessons that He learned?

3. How did the education and training of John the Baptist interact with that of Jesus? Among those who later became Jesus' Disciples, who was trained under the same teachers? Were others who were not mentioned in the Bible trained under the same teachers? Who were they and what was their relationship with Jesus?

4. What were the events that led to Jesus' travels for further training? Where did He travel, who were His mentors, and what did He learn in His travels? Was He a teacher to others at this time? How did He know where to go?

5. How did Jesus learn to stay in balance?

We certainly welcome any information that we may not have known to ask but that might be useful to us.

LAMA SING COMMENTARY

We are humbled here to be afforded this opportunity to provide the information which shall follow. That which shall be given shall be obtained primarily from the records oft called the Akasha. In order that such can be understood, do recall that many perspectives will be sought, and therefore the individuality of each perspective will contribute in terms of the influence and/or patterns which may be found in same.

TEACHERS

In the period of preparation by those who were called the Expectant Ones, or Essenes, there was the knowledge due to the preparation of certain of these to enable them to develop into that which could be called the seers or, in a manner of speaking, the prophets within their grouping; as such, this as a form of schooling, training, conditioning, and whatnot.

There were those works which were a part of Elijah's, commenced in order to provide for the vehicle which would enable these, the people who would come to the call, answering it, serving it, and seeking to open themselves. That so as God's Spirit would guide, direct and choose same, that these would be given that means by which to best serve, according to their capacity.

The School of the Prophets

So there was the early conditioning, the teaching, the references, the balancing, the strengthening of body, the purification of mind and emotion. And then the awakening of the spiritual, as a part of the schooling oft referred to as the School of the Prophets.

To varying degrees of heightening and diminishment, this School, as it could be called (or more appropriately, the Brotherhood) was greater in its influence and forthrightness, and then lesser, somewhat on a cyclic basis dependent upon the conditions, which were external from the School in the ensuing times, approximate, again, 300 years.

In those times of readying for the entry of Him, who would become King, there was the acceleration of those activities to what could be called a crescendo of sorts, wherefrom the greatest of all would also receive that unto His need and His blessing through the form and ritual of recognition. But in order that this can have continuity, let us follow this course of events…

Among those who were developed through these mechanisms, there came to be relied upon those who guided this manner of activity and that. And among these there was given the authority to yet others: some the greater, in the sense of their education and awareness, and some perceived as not so much so. Each was honored in accordance with their level of acceptance internally, much moreso than externally, for the Light could be seen by those who had opened themselves to perceive and, therefore, recognition was clearly a capacity of the grouping in total.

Here, then, there emerged strength among several of the women of this grouping and, to be sure, the authority in terms of the brotherhood and the tenets of the Essenes and such, and a mix with that of the law of the temples of the peoples of the Hebraic faith, as well. Though the interpretations were ofttimes considered different and on other occasions considered to be in violation of the Law, the spirit and truth and wisdom of these entities, the Essenes, enabled them to endure and to prepare the way for the Master's entry.

Important Essene Teachers

Now many of the teachers, as such (and rightfully, each of these entities could be considered such) obtained their skills or their uniqueness through the exacting processes of the Essenes.

The inner council was comprised of those who had obtained recognition and could demonstrate these abilities, and these were those who either did the teaching or selected those who would. See?

Judy and Others

Perhaps among some noteworthiness here is the entity known as Judy, who had, as a part of the mantle of office, some considerable authority in the close proximity to the care, and all of the activities which were later to be offered or "taught" as you would call it (put that in quotes for the most accuracy).

At the onset, then, was in some judicial capacity and evaluative capacity, along with Ruth, Salome, another Elizabeth, Jacob, Thaddeus, Marcius, and others such as this, far lesser known in their annotation in the archives or writings, but nonetheless important figures along the Essene lineage, and here incarnated. It was discerned to be a part of the cycle, which had conditionally followed the progression of the man who was known as Jesus, to become the Christ, in the evidencing to mankind.

So then, observing, caring, guiding, directing, the authority here: Judy (or Judith), Josie, Sophie, Sarah, Ruth, and the other Elizabeth all present here, to varying degrees of involvement... Editha and others such as this... Myra, and so forth... came as was the need or the opportunity to contribute and, as such, step back when not needed but close at hand.

Josie

A true joy was the tender care and love given by Josie and her blessing to purify the body, to keep it holy, as it were, to wit, she was continuously in soft gentle song. Thus, not only did she bathe the Master in the sense of cleansing the body, but bathed Him with joyous melody and song, often singing the songs and prayers, yes, but those things lightly, too, as were the custom or customs or her peoples. See?

The Twelve Maidens

So it was to come that the choice was to be delivered unto the Temple from the selection of the Maidens who were discerned to be among the most worthy, this activity at a youthful age... perhaps remarkable to some from your current reference point as early as three, four, years of age.

The development, here, was adhered to: the purity, the sanctification, and the reflection. All helped each of these Maidens to develop; and ultimately, each was contributive to the Master in their own unique way, even though Eleven were not chosen.

Mary and Joseph

Then came that time, as it was guided by the inner grouping of the Brotherhood (who consisted of the three primary seers). These counseled for the time, the ceremony at the temple, and the choice was (as is, of course, known) given by the placing of the mantle of light upon Mary as She ascended the temple steps. Then the Eleven paused, and only She continued, overlit by that form of light, the angelic messenger of God, and the pronouncement that: here is the Mother-to-be of the Master, the Light of the Earth. Then it was chosen – again, not in the human sense but in the sense of spirit anointing – and Joseph was called to the fore and given his position and role.

The Network Around Mary and Joseph

All these were, to the greater part, considered Essenes. Though some of this sect and that sect, all were firmly united, impenetrably bonded in this call, this work. For this was the manner of work to which they had prepared themselves, one and all, through many generations, many incarnations. These then, too, could be perceived and/or discerned among the brotherhood. The consideration for offering the greatest of all balance to the Master was at the forefront here. The Light of the Word of God, given through the prophets who had also gone before, was recognized and known to be honorable. And thus, God's Spirit honored this very work, or works, as had gone before, even so as there would come he who would anoint the Master and proclaim Him to those who were in those lands in those times.

Thus, as the union was complete and the ceremony, and then the waiting, there was the gathering, around and about Mary and Joseph, those who would protect, provide for, and secure their path. All of the entities in the outlying areas of the Essene groupings were advised of the activities, and the call was sent forth then to the distant lands – Persia, India, and elsewhere – that the way was being made passable and was, in fact, nigh unto open, that there should come, then, the Master.

So it began, in a sort of a multiple-faceted series of activities. The inner grouping was chosen from the other Eleven who were candidates for (as it could be said from the Essene viewpoint) *service*. It was known, in the sense of the truest Consciousness, that one who was to be with Him; it was seen. Yet, the honor and the tradition, the heritage and the prophecies, were not to be slighted, ignored, and all was given its appropriate honor, that the very best as was possible would be that which would be adhered to and followed.

Various members of the Essene groupings came to the fore here and there as it was discerned, constantly guided by those who could see and know, offering this perspective, that activity, this joy, this wonder, this challenge, and always surrounded by an impenetrable sphere of loving light. Such was the condition here, that naught could enter in. Period.

Even so, as given, the Essenes were dedicated, and when they knew that which was before them, in a sense of knowledge or wisdom and had knowledge of what to do of themselves, this they did, thoroughly. So, when the threat came against the children, their action was to protect as they knew to do, strengthening their belief in their tradition and, hence, in turn, strengthening their faith, their power in the capacity of being capable of allowing God's Spirit to flow through them.

The Teachers' Qualifications

In the Essenes' terminology, they were those who were (quote) "awakened" (end quote). And these had the inner circle care, guidance, and teaching. It was passive, not active in the sense of your current approach to education. Mindful, then, ever, of the value of example: the best teaching is by example. This they knew and followed. Their training was considerable, and their purification process began at early childhood and was the measure of whether or not they were worthy for this or any such office. Only after they had passed through the purification time did they reach that point where they were given the opportunity to expand further. With each step of the expansion and demonstration for the capacity to expand, they were given more. Thus, their individual training might be seen as much more rigid and authoritative. But remember, this was considered to be no small task or opportunity, no small responsibility. Those candidates were more demanding of themselves than any of their teachers, this from the inner knowledge, even at early age, of the import of this (as given, see).

The choice of these entities was by prophecy, by edict, and then ofttimes by affirmation from (quote) "spirit" (end quote): through a sign, a symbol, or whatnot, usually at the temple ceremonies (the Essenian temple ceremonies). They were chosen for their courage, their tenacity, their capacity for joy as a part of the qualities or qualifications. So the education was passively given by example, for the most part, and the lessons, those things, which we have given.

In Special Service to John and Jesus

So, with the entry, there was given a number of entities unto service, first, to John and, thereafter, to the Master, the man called Jesus. In this service there was the attention, first, to the care of the immediate family with, of course, the focus upon the Master, and the cleansing, the purification of the body and, thereafter, the presentation before the Temple... the circumcision, and such, according to the law; for as the Master Himself spoke: He came to uphold the Law.

Teaching Environment

Then there was the continual influence by those who were of the Essenian community and those who were involved inwardly so, see, at high levels, to the utmost degree.

Purifying and Balancing the Physical

These cleansed, these purified, these saw to the balancing of the dietary for the entire family.

Surrounding with Things of Beauty

Specifically surrounding Him with music, with poetry, and with things of beauty, as was the custom here; not those, in essence, made by man but gathered by him, in the sense that the forces of nature would be representative, unadulterated by the thought of man.

Clothing as an Empowering Signet

The garments were important, considered to be a signet of sorts, and were empowered by those who held the consciousness to so do among the inner grouping of the brotherhood. (Note here, the term brotherhood included both male and female and was not, as thought of here, to distinguish between them. It could be better stated *brethrenhood*, see?)

Note here that these were not impoverished people. They were wise, they were forthright in their dealings, they were very skilled barterers and knowledgeable of the desires of others, and dealt within their laws accordingly. Some were on the periphery, by volunteering to be such, considered to be a great sacrifice, not to be within the core or the main Essene community; and so these were looked upon highly: those who were willing to go out into the lesser thought-form of the Earth and to do that which was unto the contribution of the greater grouping. And they were most skilled in their works.

So, there was brought, also, the materials from whence to make the garments that were worn by the Master; and these were powerful, as those who prepared same used all their knowledge, and brought the energies into focus through the combinations here of patterns, of the weaving, and their own thought-form. Thus, the power of the garment itself was a sort of percursive power before the Master as a child which, in and of itself, had wondrous potentials to bring about ease... in other words, could heal.

Inundated with Love and Awe

Then Judy's influence called to the forefront other teachers and, as such, Josie became a part of the influences who loved this child dearly; not just as the Master, but for the beautiful child that He was. And as such, there could be called Sophie in that same regard. So there came to the forefront an immediate inundation of loving kindness, admiration and, of course perhaps above all else, awe. For each knew already who was this babe: the Master.

Exposure to Music and Languages

So there were brought, as time progressed and the body gathered days, weeks, months, and then years in the Earth, wondrous songs and the exposure to the instruments, and some early training in same. There was encouraged, song. There was encouraged, the harmonics of lyricism. There was encouraged, the exposure to the varying languages. Here, then, others who were colleagues of a sort to the Essenes but had their own Orders from distant lands (that's the Holy Orders, see, not the verbal order, or command); and as such, then, these began to offer to the Master sufficient stimulation to open and broaden Him... this at early ages, four, five, six.

Training of the Physical Body

There was the joy in the training of the body, and this was considered essential by the Essenes, that there would be exhibited by the others so as to be examples of the joy of being cleansed, literally and symbolically. So the bathing was given as a ceremony and was treated with some reverence. Yet, the overriding theme here was one of joy.

Encouragement of the Perceptive

There was continually the encouragement to be creative. There were small challenges (puzzles, if you will) that were brought before Him. And all would delight at the prowess, keenness, of His perception to, in the twinkling of an eye, resolve even the more difficult.

Sharpening of the Inner Being

There were others here, children of the grouping and others who had been given to the Essenes for the companionship and for the broadening, the strengthening and exposure to the varying elements, the variety, the uniqueness, of each entity. And this enabled the Master to sharpen, even here at such a youthful age, His perception of the inner being. This became a joyful sport, a game, and they would imitate and act and play.

But the body strengthening was continually a part of the doctrine, and the surrounding of the Master with those things which continually stimulated, strengthened, and supported.

Ciphering, Writing, and Patterns

There came some opportunity for ciphering, for the diagrams, for the symbols, the drawing of the letters, or the symbols that depicted a combination of letters and produced phonetics. There was the constant exposure to rhythmic patterns, cycles, breathing techniques, reflection techniques, and that sort... this mostly, though, from six to ten.

Opportunity for the Creative

There was the opportunity to work with the hands, and Joseph taught the woodworking and the skills here; not because He needed them for the labors, or unto their need (in other words, to earn) for each need was provided for, and anticipated well in advance of its expression.

Games of Purpose

There were games played, as given above. Later these became linguistic games and games of thought and reason, to offer the Master – Jesus, the man – continually a platform from whence He could expand easily and at the guidance of His own spirit and according to God's Will.

There came more and more the linguists, and more and more the artisans, and more and more the makers of song, of story, of dance, and of music. He was allowed His choice of instrument and preferred the stringed; became skilled, though did not dote on same. Took it up, mastered it quickly, and set it aside, preferring joyous song to that of something created outside of self.

The Master preferred those activities which challenged His mind and His spirit and which were joyful. Those which were merely utilitarian, He left to others; not because He sought not to labor, but that inwardly He was guided by a continual Light towards those things that would help to prepare Him in the uttermost sense to fulfill that call before Him.

Others Who Trained Jesus

It was remarkable how completely the Essenes had prepared all of this prior to its happening; and the accuracy, the veracity of the seers, the prophets, was clearly evident in the effectiveness here. There was not a concern that was not perceived sufficiently well in advance so as to be easily dealt with. Yet, as was their custom, they were steadfast in their statement of righteousness to do that which they knew to do; and after, or beyond this, to rely in utterness, with unlimited faith, upon the guidance that would come to their grouping.

Some of the Holy Maidens

As you can perceive from that as given, the main teachers of the Master in the early years, from birth to approximately the twelfth Earth year, were those of the Essenes and those of the inner core grouping, for the most part, at the onset, those who were (quote) "gifted" (end quote), in your current terminology. So these were the activities and the (quote) "training" (end quote), as provided largely by the feminine members of the Essenes, and five or six of these in the immediate vicinity of the Master being from that grouping of the twelve Maidens from which Mary was chosen.

Some from Distant Lands

As we move forward, then, we would find this continues here and there. Entities came from distant lands to present as determined appropriate, these not, as such, teaching in the sense of one, two, three, do this, do this, do this, but offering, demonstrating, exemplifying, presenting. For the spirit was always aglow within the Master, and the light in His eyes told all who came before Him, this was not one to be taught, but to be offered to, and to encourage His own expansion, growth, and all manner of such, according to that which He chose, not that which they mandated Him to learn. Quite a difference, see? But the joy was one of an electric nature, for those who were in His presence carried with them thereafter the glow of His spirit, a sort of blessing of gift.

The answer to your question, *others besides the Essenes who trained Him*, were those (as we gave) called at the appropriate time to afford that which would be moreso the common language of those entities and, as such, each brought unique capacities. There were not a great number of these from the outside, only a handful over the first twelve years. This always strictly overseen by Judy as the decision-maker, and by the entire inner council in addition to same.

Others Who Trained with Jesus

Yes, there were others who were trained, not mentioned in the Bible, under the same teachers: that just given, and others before them and, for a time, others after them, until there was no need for them to continue actively. But contrary to what is believed, the Essenes did not pass from the Earth, any more than they passed from the Atlantean to the Essenes. They merely walked a different path. They merely moved to a position of proper respect and proper regard for God's Laws and the manifestation of same throughout the Earth, waiting, holding their tenets, awakening them, rising and falling in their crest along with the flow of energies associated with the consciousness of the Earth.

But today in the Earth-time, as we speak, some Essenes are hearing these words, walking about in the Earth now. Their relationship with the Master was as followers, friends, supporters, believers. Some did not need nor seek (quote) "teaching from the Master" (end quote), in the sense that is demonstrated to the twelve Disciples, for their completeness was of a full measure, and their light only surpassed by the Master's. And so they were looked upon with love and understanding by the Master as those who had ever borne His light to His time or presentation to the Earth and, as He knew, would carry it beyond, and who are, even as we speak, yet bearing His light.

Other Children

There was continual communication with the outposts and remote locations, and with the others who would come to interact with the Master in those times ahead, and then these children came from distant lands to add to the dimension of the Master's experiences and, of course, to His personal joy.

John the Forerunner

The education of John, who was called John the Baptist, or the Forerunner (or by we here ofttimes, lovingly, as the Wooly One) was similar to that of the Master. Indeed, with Him much of the time from the early birth years to the 11th, 12th, 13th year. Much was given to both by these and by Judith until the 16th year, approximate, whereupon each was sent according to their work, their destiny, their call. So there was a separation here for a time of some several years.

Others Chosen

We do not find here (as such, in the specific sense as your question is intended) that the Disciples were trained under the same teachers. But remember, the Essenes were ever present to fulfill the prophecy, and so as they were chosen, they were provided for; they were not poor, they were not without means. Neither were many of His Disciples, and so the way was easily made passable in that regard.

So, as was the opportunity or the need or the questioning of those who were recognized as mentors, aides, and followers of the Master (but silently so), then these gave counsel where needed to the Disciples, aided them to their need, provided the garments that preserved, protected, and were of the wondrous pattern in harmony with the Master's work, each unto their own uniqueness, all twelve representing one facet, one aspect, perfectly balancing astrologically and in all respects (one from each sign).

Here, too, was the magnificence and the power made manifest in the Earth, and the Master's profoundly evident wisdom as He found and selected or chose or called upon each of the twelve. Beyond that, in honor to those who had served Him to His time of His beginning works, He chose broadly, and with loving fondness, from the Essene community those who He later dispatched to do His work, to heal in His name, as given, two by two. Most, if not all of these, were associated with the Essenes in one way or another. And those who were not directly, were totally sympathetic, as you would call it, to them, to their law, to their belief, and their faith. So in that sense, it could be said that some were trained under the same teachers. Some were the same teachers. See?

MOVING FORWARD

So, the movement up to the point where the Master began His fuller awakening, where the body was prepared, purified, sanctified, where Anna had proclaimed and prophesized... Simeon, as well, and all that sort had gone before. Now, awakened somewhat, He strode confidently into the temple, where He challenged in verbal debate. To the mirth of some, and to the consternation of others, He bested them, one by one, every one, all of them against this one child. And, here, He was found by those who were the guardians, and it was recognized that this was *the time*.

Principles, Prophecies, Powers, Perception

So, Judy herself took control here and taught the principles, the insights, the legacy, the prophecies, and many other such as were the inner actions, beliefs and points of power (as it were) carried throughout all those years in the School of the Prophets and by the Essenes, integrally as one.

Now there comes that time where her perception is clearly that there must be the expanded "work" in the knowledge that the expanded "work" (and "work" should be in quotes) would provide yet more opportunity for the purity of this Divine Spirit to manifest itself in the flesh. So there was the movement to the distant lands, and the teachings, and the counsel and such.

Training in Distant Lands

The Master was then guided by the Essenes and their supporters to the distant lands, where He was taught in the framework as we have already given it, do you see; not by rote, dogma, structure or creed, but by opportunity. Understand, this was not teaching in the sense of tradition; it was providing the opportunity for Him to express, outwardly, what was always within. Indeed, this was the observation by those respected for their decision, that all was at the ready here, or that greater opportunity should be given for this, and so forth.

As He Received, So Did He Give

As much as was given to the Master, so did He give to those, as well. Not just, as given above, in the sense of the radiant light He imparted, or the joy that He placed in their hearts; but the keen quickness of His eye and heart, and the radiance of His smile as He offered His comment, His perspective could not be measured by anything in the Earth. Nothing of the Earth value system could measure one whit to the intangible, eternal gifts from the Master.

Much of these travels and the (quote) "teachings of same" (end quote), involved opportunities to exercise, much as a performer or an artisan who was destined for a grand performance, for example, or some such work of considerable demand upon them would exercise, strengthen, prepare the instrument of their body, mind, and spirit to be as highly tuned as possible. But in the journeys to the distant lands, He as much bore those of those lands gifts as He was intended to receive gifts or blessings from them.

The Best of the Best Went Before and With Him

Judy always saw to the bearing forth of the symbolic gesture according to the doctrine, the teaching, and the belief of each place of rest. The entourage was considerable but nearly invisible to the casual observer, who would not recognize this or that entity dressed as a merchant or a herder or whatnot to be what they truly were. Among the most powerful of the inner Essene core grouping were dispatched with the Master. The best of the best went before Him, at His sides, and behind. No quarter, no approach was left without observation. Was this necessary? Certainly not. Was this their role, their gift, their heritage, their belief? Utterly. And they fulfilled it to the letter, to the jot and tittle of same.

There were always those glad times around the campfire when the sacrament had been fulfilled, the offering, the prayer, the song, the exchange and such. Then there came the times of great joy, where discussions would carry on for many hours. For here, lured by the brightness of the campfire, as was the custom, any traveler could join, and they could participate to the degree of their belief, or not. But the custom, the tradition was, all were welcome by a traveler's campfire, and this was fulfilled. (It would appear we have aroused some response from the Earth, with a note of loving humor.)

Just so, then, as these journeys continued, they followed the routes and much of the activities as have already been given elsewhere, of course, as is known quite extensively through Edgar [Cayce], but through many others, as well, whose righteousness is not questioned here but honored, and so we give the further commentary to augment same in the primary sense but to also respond to your questions.

WHAT HE LEARNED IN HIS TRAVELS

The literal events that led to the Master's travels for further training were, we believe, sufficiently given above. It was part of the preparation, the plan, by the Essenes, considerably prior to His entry. And thereafter, it was a part of the prophecy to be fulfilled and a part of His chosen work.

He was not told to go; He was offered the choice. And He chose. For His awareness was not clouded one whit, and He wanted to bear His word to them as much as to make their consciousness a part of His, that He would speak to all of the Earth as gained through the interactions with these, the major other aspects or perspectives of the Earth in those times.

Persia with Junner & Phe-El and Others

A little-perceived point here, that in Persia, He gave truth and insight and considerable teaching to those who were the disciples of the leaders there. And so, as gained from Junner in Persia and from Phe-El [phonetic] in Persia, and others like them, there came their disciples, and He unto them meted out according to their openness. He learned their song, their custom. He participated in these. He became one with them. He learned how they conditioned their body to endure. He learned how they purified themselves from thoughts of limitation. And He gave greater measure than He received.

What they offered Him were the best of their wisdoms and teachings, the jewels of their collective heritage spiritually, mentally, and philosophically. What they demonstrated was how they applied these according to their law, their heritage, their custom. Remember, this is one of the five races of man as expressed in the Atlantean times. He honored them, all five. Not one was overlooked.

Egypt

Then in the Egyptian, there were other such but similar activities. He learned here through the demonstration from these entities, much in the same manner as in the Persian: the control of the elements; the mental in terms of a means of communicating with the forces primal; the demonstration of how these entities could manipulate matter, form, and its expression; and their skill at healing, and their marvelous manipulation of the senses and all that sort, so as to make them in command of themselves.

These things He observed, and He used their techniques and also gave them the underlying truth to each step, so that theirs was the gain... that now, they not only could do, and did not have to pass down just the how-to, but why, how did it manifest, where did it come from within the body?

The Distant Eastern

There was much given and taken from the distant Eastern, who sent their emissaries, as well: the chakras, the energy centers of the body, the seven churches, the seven centers, the vibrational energies as could be transformed or directed as one made themselves one with the Spirit which created them. This, of course, was within Him from the onset. So, He carried them, as they demonstrated yet a step and another and another, beyond their current knowledge. Primary here, as given through Edgar [Cayce], Car-Gle-On [phonetic] and others, as well... Fees [phonetic] was here... Phebes [phonetic] was here... and as such, many of the others from the distant Eastern. These came and gave the symbology, the parallels, the paradoxes, those things which were the counter and counter-balance, those things which could ever be called upon from within to meet anything on the outer.

Did He not know these? Of course. But what they gave was their perspective, their interpretation, and how they made these manifest. Here again, He presented the Law, the Universal Law, upon which all of these as actions and reactions were based. And He taught the responsibility. He observed them in their passiveness as they came from the high places, and He gave to them in His activeness.

They tested their position, their philosophy, against His principles, and it was good. So, two great polarities did come together here, and from same, His work was foundationalized; not only in what He did and said, but in the bringing together, in the primal force or expression of His principles as He was prophesied to manifest, and those principles which were passive and supported all expression. The balance was made whole and complete and perfect and, thus, the Earth was open. The Master was utterly opened unto His service. See?

UPON HIS RETURN

After the return and from the Persian, there was the call to return to the homeland, which was accomplished. Then the joining with John again, and the grand celebration in the sense of the Essenes, not by Jesus nor John, for their work was in motion and the studies became specific unto each one's works, much moreso than ever before.

Exchanging Knowledge

There came all manner of people – scholars, those of wisdom from the great Alexandrian libraries – to this outpost, to (we believe it would be your south-southeast, yet near the river in the delta) where the Essenes had prepared a sort of sanctuary, a place that they controlled, a center which was controlled by them according to their teachings. So, much of the knowledge contained in the Library and many of those who came from all parts of all lands were to come to pass before the Master and to exchange to Him, from Him, and together joyous knowledge and insights. There were many festivities, and there were many serious (as you would call them), if not somber, activities. These were opportunities for the Master to strengthen Himself, to test Himself against those properties of His choice. Was He not perfect within? Yes. You are perfect within, as you hear this; your life in the Earth is your testing, chosen by you, selected by you. These works that we are speaking of were no different… directed and chosen by the Master.

He was made knowledgeable of the varieties of means of communication through these activities. And for the four-plus years in total spent in the Egyptian (approximate), these means of communication were made known to Him. Thus, it was easily possible that He could then, thereafter, reach out in any manner to express to any entity in their tongue, that all would understand.

Teaching What He Knew and Learned

He prepared the way for the future. He guided those who came, who had seen; those who were called the Wise Men, who in some respects anointed Him at birth, were here to receive from Him, now, teachings that He held within Himself and that were not upon any document, any writing. He took them from spirit and put them into expression. He demonstrated to them, that they might learn, and from their knowledge they might carry this forward, translate it, protect it, mold it so that it would be preserved intact as a living spirit or essence, in a variety of works, each chosen according to the intent and purpose of the individual. He guided them, that they would know how to guide others.

He called upon those forces, of which He had now diverse knowledge from those who He befriended in His distant travels, and He exemplified these, to the amazement of the scholars, teachers, seers, prophets or prophets-to-be who all came in an orderly manner to be before Him. And in the journeys back to His homeland here and there, He gave and brought much in the sense of the connection, if you could call it or consider it such. For mind is the builder, and just as sure as it has oft been given in the Earth, here and elsewhere, it was known then.

So, to turn back to the questions for a moment, yes, He was a teacher to others at this and most all of these times. After leaving the premises of Judy, He actually began the moreso His own teaching than His own study. But there was, and is, the respect for the uniqueness of each, so this was encouraged as a part of the study and works, the travels in all these lands and among all these disciples or emissaries or teachers from the diverse places.

Among those things which He (quote) "learned" (end quote), were astrology, philosophy; the expressions and manifestations of the varying forms of theosophy from the diverse places; the purification of the mind and emotion, that those things as illusions in the Earth could not have any detrimental effect to His works, not to Him but to His works; the capacity to move into harmony, oneness, with all things and, therefore, to be in command of them, be they elemental or cellular in their nature (living things, see).

He was taught by those who held the prophesies of their own lands according to their perspective of same, and He offered those qualifications in return and His suggestions on how each of these entities might carry back to their peoples a better understanding, and taught them how to demonstrate the truth of what they were offering. (A number of these who became noteworthy in later years will find their heritage based in these interactions between the Master and emissaries of their lands. Emphasis here: India, Persia, and the Far East.)

The Carpathians and other such of the high lands were highly contributive, as well, for their mental acuity, their clarity of sight, the capacity for patience and understanding were good opportunities for the Master to sort of exercise these qualities within Himself. It is written that an entity's quality of song is enhanced when they are joined in song by others. And so, this is what is meant here. See?

The choices on the part of the Master as to who to interact with, and earlier where to travel, were always decisions made by Himself from within. But He always sought the counsel, and listened to it carefully and lovingly, by the Essenes, by their seers and such, and He continually regarded all of these with honor. So, His knowledge of where to go came from the Essenes, and He accepted their preparation joyfully and honored it. Though at any point in any activity or journey, His was the greater capacity to perceive, if that was His wish. But His faith was a part of the strengthening here, and He placed it in God, whom He recognized as being the Father of these wonderful peoples called the Essenes. So, as He recognized them as children of God, they were immediately also accepted as His brethren and, therefore, without limit. Thus, His faith, His trust in them, was perfect.

The Essenes gave to Him, by their presence, from birth through at least the sixth Earth year, such environmental conditions and joys that it was evermore from here that His most principled, most foundational, capacity to remain in balance was based. If a tree begins with its roots firmly and deeply in the Earth, then, as it grows, so does its foundation become stronger. The Master was and is firmly rooted through the grace, through the loving blessings of God's Spirit manifested in His children, the Essenes.

So in all, the Master gave equally as He received, if not greater. The teachings in all these places and through all these entities was truly a gift to the teacher. Whether they were recognized as an entity of great wisdom from a distant land, or an Essene whose life had been a continual demonstration of faith and joy, he looked upon them all equally.

Staying in Balance

Mary, His mother, surrounded Him with the balance of Her soul's harmony with Him, perfect in nature... Elizabeth, whose John was to play such a role, gave equally so, and honored Him... Josie, whose love knew no limitation... Editha, who revered Him as a child and as a teacher. And it could go on and on here, and there would be perhaps many names (and from those names other names, no different than many of you having the name that you are called, and then the familiar name from those close to you, so let not these things embroil you, but look to the Spirit, as we pray we have offered here).

4 - John and The Essenes

CHANNEL/AL MINER: In this work we ask for information on the entity John the Forerunner, or John the Baptist, as he was called after his death. From Biblical accounts, we know little of the life of John, or Jochanan, his Hebrew name.

SPONSOR'S QUESTION:

1. Please tell us of his life essentially after he began his ministry and teaching:

2. Please give a description of his physical appearance and the more obvious characteristics of his personal expression, both of which appear to have been very unique and perhaps somewhat wild as was his manner of dress. And, did you really call him "the woolly one"?

3. Did he have such a unique fondness of the forces of nature and of being out in the wilderness, roughing it? What was his lifestyle like? Was it influenced by his problems with the orthodox priesthood after renouncing his birthright position as a high priest in order to become an outcast, as Edgar Cayce called it?

4. What was John's teaching like? What was the difference or change to Yeshua's teachings?

5. Please tell us about his past lives. Was he influenced by incarnations in India, in which he obtained mastership through difficult means... asceticism and denial, harsh physical discipline, perhaps like a fakir or a shaman?

6. Then there's the incarnation as the prophet Elijah or Elias, who also established or restructured the "School of the Prophets" that had been founded by Samuel, based on Melchizedek's teachings. Did John consciously know and/or accept that he was Elijah? One Gospel reports that he denied it when

he was asked. Why? Had John also come as the Forerunner in several other incarnations of the Master

7. What was meant when Jesus said, "The least in the kingdom of Heaven was greater than John the Baptist"? And "Among them that are born of women there has not risen a greater than John the Baptist"?

8. Why did John doubt the Master at some point? Which events and/or teachings made him think that Yeshua might not be the Messiah? After he had sent his emissaries to Jesus in order to directly ask him whether or not they would have to wait for another, was the message he received enough to convince or assure him? And when he had regained his faith, did he then tell his own Disciples to leave him and to follow the Master?

9. How large was John's following? Did most of them become Christians (did most of the Essenes, for that matter)? What was his position within the Essenes, or of his group among other factions? According to Cayce, John was more Essene than Jesus. Was Jesus perhaps perceived as being a bit too outgoing or liberal?

10. Did John also heal, cast out demons, and perform miracles? Or was he primarily a channel for information?

11. Did John choose his untimely death, perhaps because of self-denial? Did he have the choice to remain and walk with the Master, side-by-side physically?

12. John appears to be present with you. You have said that his spirit is a part of these very works, and that there is no small part of these works directly attributed to John. Is he a member of your group, Lama Sing?

13. As a powerful companion soul to the Master, he was and is about the work of preparing the way for him, and it is rumored that John has already returned to the Earth in physical body. Is this correct? If yes, is that to mean that the return of the Master is very near at hand, perhaps even within the next ten to twenty years?

We thank you very much, Al and the Lama Sing group.

LAMA SING COMMENTARY

We find that the ministry, as such, was quite simplistic, very straightforward, and philosophically basic in terms of a combination of what could be called the Essenian teachings and beliefs, a combination of Eastern teachings that were given through the teachers who schooled John in those earlier years of childhood, and others which were of course given unto John directly by the Angelic Host and those who are, even still here, gathered about these works, seeking to guide, to offer enlightenment, ever in God's name.

SUMMARIZING JOHN

John was and is paradoxical in this lifetime as John, and in numerous others. Paradoxical in the extent that there could be on the one hand such a compassion, such an attitude of yielding or gentleness, so as to think the man never capable of anything that was of conflict or contrast. Yet, when confronted with what he considered to be a violation of God's Laws, there was little that could be done to restrain him. In many respects, he considered himself a protector of God's Laws and of God's Forces, His Spirit expressed in nature.

His compassion for nature, his relationship to the forces of nature, was (and is) long-standing. Therefore, this must, you see, include all of humankind, the peoples who were in those times, as well.

Physical Appearance

The physical appearance, as you have questioned, was that largely of a staturely, almost intimidating, figure; not so much from the size or form of his body, but from the literal manner of his bearing... the eyes, the expression, and the ease with which he moved through practically all things. (He found it as easy to accomplish movement into and out of a city as he did the ease with which he traversed many miles of wilderness.)

The Wooly One

The stature was approximately an inch or so less than the Master, and about the breadth of what you would consider to be a laborer, or one of physical labor in the Earth at present... in other words, broad to the upper section of the body, though not overly so. Not excessively muscular, the frame just moreso broad (actually, more lean than thick).

He wore his hand-woven garments which he so fondly gathered from the animals, who came to him freely – and only pulling the hair, see, not to the loss of the animal, never such – but these he would fashion. He would gather all manner of things and make them into garments, some of them of such bulk so as to make him look, literally, woolly. Hence, the phrase coined, "the Woolly One."

Fastidious, in terms of personal cleanliness, but this was a derivation of the Essene teaching. Strict to diet, strict to meditation and prayer.

He always sought to keep himself – body, mind, and spirit – as pure as possible. When water was not present, he would bathe with the Earth itself. Hence, he often had the appearance of being unclean, but he was not. This was his way. See?

The hair was thick, heavy, both facial and head, and somewhat so darker than most upon the body. But this, perhaps, due to the elements and nature causing this as a sort of reaction to the needs thereof, for the temperatures were very dramatically extreme.

Manner of Dress

Manner of dress was several-fold. When not amongst the peoples, his dress would be as suited him, sometimes handwoven garments, as indicated above, from fibers and hairs and whatnot. He would weave them himself just to see what it felt like to wear those energies, those colors, those essences. He was as curious to the animal kingdom in that regard as he was to the peoples, and perhaps even curious to himself; just as quick to laugh, as he was to judge and make a statement based upon his judgment (those things were very powerful, see). When with the peoples, he was brought garments suitable for his ministry and works, and these he accepted.

His Staff

He was also known to carry a great staff. It was said that the staff was magical unto itself. It was also said that it was given to him by Michael, himself – the Archangel – and that in the giving, there was placed upon him a mantle of service, and that the power of God's authority was resident in the staff. The staff was feared as much as John. Well, perhaps feared a bit too strong; respected, the better. He often was without it, to the curiosity of some, and he would never divulge why he did not have it on certain occasions and other times he did, nor where it would be when he did not have it. Some stated he simply made it appear and disappear as it suited him, moreso as a lark.

Lifestyle

Dedicated to frequent long sojourns, as many as three to six months in the wilderness. This, to him, was a place of peace and oneness with God, and all things of nature seemed to be in harmony with him wheresoever he would go.

At One with Nature

It is written here that often the animal kingdom would bring to him many things unto his needs, and he would tend them and heal them and do such works. These were primarily the focus of his healing works. With nature and from nature, giving and receiving both. His focus was teaching and, as you call it, serving as a channel of blessings.

Often in the highlands and in the deserts he could be met by a passing caravan, whom he would greet with spontaneous vigor, almost as though (and many would say this) he would appear from nowhere and leave just as mysteriously. He would follow whatever his intuition prompted him to follow. He would just as easily follow a group of wild animals as they migrated, as he would follow a caravan, just for the lark of it, the fun of it.

He was also somewhat of a skilled artisan; clever with the hands, clever with the energies, capable of creating works of some beauty, as well as his notorious woolly garments.

Personality

Powerfully decisive, powerfully evaluatory. Noted for his fondness, like the Master, of children. Many would, when they knew that he was camped nearby, bring their children to him, and he would sing with them, tell stories, dance, and all that sort, as with the Master. But this was the Essene way. Children were considered gifts from God: pure, simple, and utterly truthful. Powerfully inquisitive. Often challenging. He was not well regarded by the orthodox; quick to speak his mind about them and their tendency to gather power and wealth, pointing out that a man or woman of God need naught of the physical, for God provided all to those who served in His name, and he evidenced this, to the amazement of all he encountered!

As an Essene

Lifestyle in the sense of your current Earth time, very different. Not predictable, not rigid and, thus, some Essenes regarded him with question. But then, similarly did they (some of them) question the actions and works of the Master, even though they knew full well who He was.

John was as likely to walk into one of their ceremonies, even the holiest of holy, sit down in his woolly garments, handmade, and sing a song in the midst of a ceremony, disrupting all, except for the children, who would laugh and gather about him. And he would be chastised, to which he would answer, "Thinkest thou God prefers thy rattling, or my song? I think the latter." At which point, he would sing all the louder, joined, of course, in mighty chorus by the children and the giggles of those who loved him dearly. Few challenged him among the Essenes, for they knew him as one with the Master, and as that one who would anoint the Master and fulfill the Prophecy. Therefore, he was often, by those of authority, the moreso tolerated. But even in these who judged him the most harshly, there was a sense of admiration and love. For it was difficult not to love him when he was in those states of expression.

Outcast by Dictums

In and about the temples he was, more oft than not, driven off forcibly, for he would speak aloud, vociferously, his opinions, and they didn't very often fit well with those of the priests. Although the basic tenets were the same, and he, too, honored the Law, he spoke of equality and simplicity, and this, of course, caused some to be looked upon by the peoples with great question, a situation which would be unheard of, were it not for John. This was, incidentally, his undoing. Did not renounce the priesthood, as such, to become an outcast; he was an outcast by their terms and by their dictums. So, the birthright, as such, was irrelevant, in a manner of speaking (given with a note of loving humor). But even these respected, and even feared, John, for they knew John to have certain powers. Though none knew of him misusing them, none wanted to be the first to find that out

As given above, John's position among the Essenes (taken from the timeframe you stated at the onset above, after he began his teaching and ministry, we believe) was mixed. It depends upon whom you talk to. All regarded him with honor, but some at close quarters and others at arm's length, if you catch the meaning implied by that.

Comparing John with Jesus

John was, perhaps, in some respects viewed by some to be more the Essene than Jesus. But most who viewed John that way didn't know him all that well. They knew of him, they heard his teachings when he chose to be among them. Beyond this, they didn't know the John of song and merriment, of dance and frolic, the John who gathered around the hundreds and hundreds of campfires in the midst of the wilderness.

Personality

We couldn't say that Jesus was a bit too outgoing. Jesus knew the Law because He was and is the Law. He did not see according to the sight of mankind; He saw according to the spirit. It mattered not where He saw a spirit in need or a light that could be fueled; He went to it, whether that was in a tavern or in a temple. So, we could conclude here that in some respects John was moreso the Essene. Not quite as strict as you might think, but yes, in many ways more strict than the Master. But then, remember: the Master is the Christ, see; John was and is growing.

Teaching

The teaching was directly parallel to that of the Master. Though not quite so demonstrative as the Master's own actions, teachings, and works, there were continued demonstrations invoking the awareness of others. And this was one of the powerful, if not magnetic, qualities about John that drew so many to him. He was taught, just so as the Master, many of the ancient teachings. Some of these were considered to be magical and whatnot, but to John they were simple truths expressed through the eyes and minds of those who went before him. He took the best of these and cast aside the lot that were not, according to his assessment.

He had knowledge of what could be considered the ancient teachings, these then given by the Eastern teachers who came forth to teach during childhood. And these were used often to manipulate matter when it was in accord with his guidance. This was not done idly, but only so as John considered it as a part of a mission or commission, which he heard and followed without question. There were those teachings that were from John that involved the Creative Forces, though these, for the most part, involved the individual. There were those teachings from John which were directly channeled and, therefore, while they were of John, they were not from John. See?

JOHN'S INCARNATIONS

In the past lives, there were those activities, often, seeking to be a forerunner of the Master's entry. Unfortunately, many of these did not become fulfilled, not in the physical. And so it was that he was a very difficult taskmaster to himself, and often would judge himself even as John, as he did in previous lives, and demand more and more from his own life, his own consciousness. Hence, he would often take his odysseys into the wilderness, to purge himself of the energies of what you might call mass-mind thoughts.

With the Master in Atlantis; with the Master in Egypt; with the Master in Persia; with the Master in India. He was also in India on several occasions, as your latter question inquires; in Tibet; in South America; in North America; and perhaps had many more literal physical incarnations in the Earth than did the Master. So one can quickly conclude here that John did not always precede the Master, even though he would often attempt to do so in one curious way or another.

Incarnations Obtaining Mastership

Some of his meaningful works were in Persia and in India (or Inja [phonetic]), in other lands, to be sure, but because the questions ask of same, we can respond. Yes, there were experiences in India which were extremely dedicated, almost to a fault, almost to a point where he would border on death and, just at the last moment, pull himself back into the Earth. We find from the records, that this was by design: to eliminate the fear of, and to familiarize his awareness of, the passage called death. This he accomplished, and was able to do many wondrous works as a fakir or shaman, and a healer in those times.

He also appeared in China in early times, and studied the flow of energy, the manipulation of energy, and the direction of same, and all that manner of such. In the South American, there was the profound study of what would be called sacred geometry, the symbology and use of tones and energies for the transmutation and transformation of elemental expression. There were, in the North American, a number of incarnations which involved both the true Americans and, later, the (currently as defined) Americans. There were incarnations in England; among the Crusades, in France; in the Steppe or what would be called highlands of Russia; and so on and so forth.

This soul, then, curious and adventuresome, always seeking to serve the Word of God but doing so to the utter limits of that definition; not crossing over the Word of God but exploring it fully. Comparatively, the Master followed a path of incredible balance and ease, not choosing this sort of involvement. For the Master had this awareness totally within himself; John was unwilling to accept without proving to himself that he was worthy each time.

Self-denial was one of the limitations here. John's greatest struggles, perhaps, were with John, not so much the Earth… His regard for the Earth was categorically clear. His understanding of the forces of nature, the expression of God's spirit in same, was clear. He was capable of working with or being in harmony with these forces and, thus, cooperating and directing them according to the Law, see, as John knew of same at some levels. But would not accept consciously, the possibility of being Elijah or, more accurately, Elias.

Attempting to respond to your questions in the direct sense, yes: John, in a number of incarnations, came to prepare the way. But not alone; there were many others. John would be the first to emphasize that he was but one of many.

UNDERSTANDING JESUS' WORDS ABOUT JOHN:

The Least in the Kingdom of Heaven …

The first comment by the Master regarding the least-most in the Kingdom of our Father in Heaven as greater than John was to point out in that commentary that spirit is pure, spirit is great; and that in spirit there is the knowledge eternal, the force vitae, the essence of life itself. In the body (in that commentary) is the temporary, the limited, the focused, the finite. That was the reference here.

Among Them That Are Born of Women …

The reverse of same is found in the second statement, that

in terms of those born of woman into the Earth, greater than John was not in existence. In other words, John was considered by the Master equal to the greatest of all, and none were greater. He also honored John in this respect, to associate him with the great prophets and teachers of old, in the knowledge that John was some of these.

The emphasis here was, on the part of the Master, to make clear that John in body was, compared to John in spirit, very minimal. But John in his consciousness of the sum of his being had no greater counterpart in the Earth. See?

Curious Question

We find your questions regarding John's possible doubt of the Master curious. Knowest thou not that John and the Master studied together as children? John saw clearly the Master's works as a child, and knew them, and knew the Master! Only during those years of the Master's travel, where John remained and studied with the Eastern teachers in the sacred schools, were they separated.

Fulfilling the Prophecy

Therefore, the comments by John were the moreso to fulfill the prophecy, for as with the traditional Essene teaching, John and the Master both attempted to fulfill the Law, not to quarrel with it, and to honor the prophets, and so they did. John's question that was dispatched by his colleagues (or, as you call them, disciples) was to fulfill this in the knowledge that, so as this was to be done in the manner that it was done, it was the awakening, the opening, the beginning of the work. It was, more or less, a communication between the spirit of the Master and the spirit that is John, that: the work shall now begin.

In the Earth, it appears there was the questioning. But then, how else would this be made known, made public; for the followers of John were not sworn to secrecy, and each place they rested they told with excitement, with jubilation He is come! Thus, the way was prepared and made open. Hence, this is by which John is called, even in your current time. The message or answer received from the Master was irrelevant. But it fulfilled the prophecy, and it awakened the peoples and prepared the way.

Teaching

John's questioning of the Master when they met at the stream was for the similar purpose, for there was a great gathering waiting to be with John, to be healed through baptism of spirit, and to learn – and laugh – with him. (He wasn't quite as strict and such as is currently documented. Had they documented some of his commentary and some of his antics, those works wouldn't have appeared to most as being quite as spiritual as one would expect them to be.) John's comments were pointed, but loving, gentle, and always in a manner that those who were listening and/or observing could clearly understand.

The Master's teachings were given in a manner which was timeless, given to endure in the knowledge that, though they would be recorded and altered and abbreviated, the sacred code would remain within same for all those who have eyes to see and ears with which to hear. This he knew. See?

So there were differences. But even so, one could find remarkable point of humorous similarity in the quickness of both to gather with the lowliest amongst the lands, apparently, more often than not preferring those to the highborn or those with wealth or stature.

Jesus was the moreso tolerant and accepting and loving of those highborn and with wealth and power; John was only barely so… unless their spirit shone clearly from them, he had little to do with them. Those who labored with their hands and hearts and whose light shone pure from them, he loved; but those who were not so, he had little time to abide with.

JOHN'S FOLLOWING

It is difficult to respond to your question regarding the size of John's group, or (as you called it) following. For, from his perspective, he did not consider those he lived with, and shared with and taught and so on, to be his.

Numbered in the Thousands

From the standpoint of the true intent of your question, there were thousands who John met and broke bread with and sat around campfires with. John was often, as we gave above, known to just appear... to walk into an encampment and seat himself comfortably at fireside with groupings, caravans, and such, to the amazement and shock of those who were gathered around same, for they guarded their perimeter carefully because of marauders and such. Yet, John would simply walk up to the campfire, unseen and unheard, until he wished it.

So, many heard his perspective of Truth, of the Law, and many heard his laughter and song. See? And many who returned to their distant homelands told of this Woolly One, who appeared and joined them and taught and sang, and vanished as quickly as he came.

He was never reluctant to accept gifts or blessings, but was always the first to offer them. He would provide travelers with all sorts of delicacies from nature. Precious oils, herbs, medicines, honey, compotes, and all that sort. He carried great swaths of garment in which he carried many different pouches and such and gave them freely, expecting naught in return. But when he was given gifts, he accepted them. John was a purveyor of truth.

He was also a purveyor of merriment and mischief. But when he spoke of the Messiah, the Son of God, he did so with fire inward and in his eyes.

Many Became Enlightened

So we could number his "grouping" (and best put that in quotes or he'd be offended even now, see)... but those he had influence, contact, with and those whose lives he impacted positively, were in the thousands. Many of these did become Christians. Many of them became something different than this; they became enlightened unto themselves. For John did not only teach the Word, he taught others to find the Word within themselves, and to hear it no matter what tongue or what manner was used to convey same.

John knew that the Law was perfect for all entities, and that those who might not find their way through the Light of the Master in that lifetime would ultimately find their oneness with the Christ by the paths that would be offered to them in their own land, or in their own nature. Wisely, he fueled this in many. So, he is yet, in the current time, regarded highly in many of these distant lands.

Followers Were Held in High Regard

As you look at those who were the inner circle of John's companions, or (to stretch, this and hope he doesn't find offense at same) his followers, there were several dozens. Some closer, some a bit more removed, but we'd say a lot of seventy-odd, all of which, except for a handful, then turned and followed the Master. Many of these, if not most of them, were those who the Master sent out, two by two. (Remember that?)

The followers of John were held with some regard. The followers of John were healers, but for the most part, they healed with knowledge of the Law. They healed with many of the herbs and potions and compotes and such that John gave them by the bagful, as though he had some sort of mysterious factory somewhere in the wilderness (which of course, he did not). These were known to heal and cure maladies and dis-ease, and so, many of John's followers were looked upon with reverence. They were very effective, but they knew the Law as John knew it; they knew that within nature, there could be found the answer to any need, and such as this. So, in some respects, they could be thought of as counterparts in pharmacopeia or herbology, in naturopathic, and such.

John taught them to see such as the forces, the energies. He taught them to enter those forces and manipulate them. But not so as the Master did; this was according to the Law and to the natural laws of the realm called Earth. John was a bit of a mystic in some respects and knowledgeable of the ancient teachings and the old arts, and wasn't afraid to use them.

We have spoken in past of the relationship between Judy and John. Here, there is a love that is profound; in the recognition of the one to the other, is a great light. Wherever you find John serving the Master, a step or two distant from that in any direction, you will most assuredly find Judy, as well.

Ministry

John did not, as such, cast out demons and perform miracles; John, in many respects, became one with nature, knew it, and took from nature its gifts. Tthese, of course, were miracles unto themselves. The Master needed naught to do His works, although, note that he often used some of the elements in nature to strengthen His works for the recipient's purposes or needs, not His own. John the moreso reliant upon these; the Master, of course, was not.

John was primarily, perhaps, a channel of blessings. But not just of information… of love, of laughter, and of many different things.

Overall, then, it would be John who would state that he was and is not special. But in the sense or spirit of your asking these questions, he is certainly at the very least, now and always in the past, willing. And that is a significant thing. For in the willingness or in the confirmation according to the Law of Free Will, John will always be, if not the first, one of those, to answer a call from the Master, almost to a fault.

When His Work Was Complete

Some of the key disciples knew that, when the time was appropriate, they would leave John and follow the Master. Most did not [know], so this came as a startling revelation and created a great conflict within many, for so many had come to love the way of John, yet knew and loved what they were taught by John as the works which were associated with the

Master. Once with the Master, they were inundated with the Master's power of love, truth, and compassion, and His spirit overlit them with abundance. John was not quite capable of this.

In a manner of speaking, the decisions in life are the right of Free Will for each and every entity. To the extent that this is valid – and that it surely is – it could be stated that John did choose his untimely death; in part because of self-denial, in part because he was always expecting more from himself each and every Earth day.

Not Without Fault

Not without fault, mind you. His greatest fault was his own self-judgment and such as this. And his strong expectation that those who rose in authority should be examples of the Law, and this infuriated him when he saw them doing the opposite. It was that, that was primarily his downfall.

In the latter years of his teaching, just prior to the ceremony with the Master, he became much more vocal and much more predictable. Whenever there was an event of noteworthiness, a celebration by those in authority (the Romans or whatnot) he was present, appearing in the midst of a crowd and seemingly vanishing with the same remarkable ease. Therefore, there was always among the guard and among the priests (you could call them the temple workers) a lookout for John. It was said that before he appeared, there would be the odor of the wildflowers and wild honey that many claimed saturated his garments (humorously given).

A terrible taskmaster, John was always analyzing and criticizing and judging himself, questioning his own motives, questioning his actions. But this was very much an attitude that was general in the Essenes: self-denial and self-condemnation. The Master tried often to convince John that, in order to truly be a temple of God's Light and love, he must love himself. Yet, John often receded into his own condemnation. These were things that contributed to his downfall.

A Part of These Works

But most of all, we should think here, he knew his work was complete. Yes, he could have remained. Yes, he could have walked with the Master. Yes, the works might have been, even the moreso, memorable. And perhaps many other things that we are told clearly here not to comment about, yes, these things were and are possible.

But the Master is the Christ; John, a follower, one who loved and does love and is loved by the Master. John would stand at the back and allow all others to come forward. That is the nature of that soul. Yes, he instructed his followers, except for a handful, to leave and follow the Master, but many of these knew that. They only awaited that day, that time, and for John to speak the words. Yes, it is accurate that John is a part of these works here. It is his spirit that is, to a great degree, the vehicle by way of which these works, cumulative – present and future – might be given.

LOOK TO THE LIGHT

It would be to his displeasure to comment much more than this, for his direction to all of you will always be: Look to the Christ, look to the Master: There is the Light, the Promise, and the Way! So we shall honor that intent and philosophy that is held so warmly in the spirit of that called John. This does not necessarily mean that the Master will return very soon, within the next ten to twenty Earth years. But were it John's right to decide, it would most assuredly be so! John and so many of the others – Peter, Paul, Andrew, Mathias, Samuel, Jacob, Anna, Judy, and on and on (and we could name a few of you, as well, dear friends) – were it unto these and their right to so do, the way would be opened and made passable, and the Master would be among you in the passage of a cycle little known to you but soon to be discovered. And that would be within an approximate... Well, we're told not to state that. But yes, within that time frame as you have stated it: ten to twenty Earth years.

So now you have this information on John. We have given it carefully and with some reverence, and some caution because, among our grouping here, to single one out is not the nature of a good worker. John would be the first to emphasize that this is not a good thing to do. But because we are pledged to serve in the manner that we serve through this, our Channel, we have complied.

But mark you well: Do not revere the name of that called John the Baptist, John the Beloved, John the Forerunner (and on and on, as he has literally dozens of names and such); but look into your own heart and see what is there. It is equal unto John or Paul or Saul or Jacob or Benjamin or Enoch or Adam (which is the same as the Christ) and all of these, for has He not told you this, Himself?

That which you find within, then, that is of this eternal Light. Unto the equal of the honor that you give to this Light within yourself, certainly give same unto John, in the knowledge that, so doing, he will equally honor you and bless you in return in the name of his Brother, the Christ.

Not much else to tell here. As we perceive it, John was and is, like so many, aware enough to hear, to see, and to know the Master to be the Christ; and open enough, willing enough, to serve with and for Him. But he is not alone in this, nor is he greater or lesser than any of the others. That we might add, will include some of you who will hear these words. So you might (with a note of paradoxical humor) see how well you can deal with such recognition. We mean that with love and with humor.

Here is an important point, which is a part of John's continued works, his continued efforts: Begin where you are, with who and what you are, and love that. Grant yourself God's grace. Forgive yourself. Be patient and have long-suffering towards self. For if the temple of God's Light is not within you, then where shall it be found? As the Master gave unto Peter, "This is the Rock upon which I shall build my church." His meaning was, the purity of his spirit.

CLOSING COMMENTS

In the hearts and minds of those who call themselves the Children of God is the potential of a Light so beautiful so as to make all things well.

It is the Christ who urges lovingly, who lifts up with an embrace of love, this perspective of your true beauty. And it is His word, His teaching, that will be the path of greatest joy and ease unto which, if you follow same, you will become one with that Light.

5 - *The Baptism of Jesus*

LAMA SING COMMENTARY

While the sun's rays cannot be seen as yet, there is the subtlety of a glow against the backdrop of an indigo sky, dotted with the tiny lights of celestial bodies beginning to fade. Here and there, a few sounds can be heard as creatures of the Earth call out, as though they, themselves, are summoning forth the entrée of yet another new day on Earth.

Here, gathered before the traditional place, there are already a goodly number. And more can be seen walking along the river's edge. Far away, there can be seen one... two small groupings, moving slowly, clutching their garments to their body in the pre-dawn's chill. But on the periphery are those who are His.

In the midst of those gathered, many who are a part of the Essenes move about, tending to various needs, encouraging, joining with small groupings in prayer, generally spreading their good spirit, sharing their light with those who would have it. Of particular note are the teachers and Maidens, for the hour is come. And they are aware that the work shall this day begin.

We can see him, now, striding over a small knoll with a small group of his followers. His staff seems to glisten, though there is little or no light. Yet, so it does. His hair is long, and the pre-dawn wind blows it about. Those with him pull their garments tighter, and yet he pays this chill no mind. His eyes are fixed upon the gathering and the gentle slope leading into the water's edge, as though no one else were present, so is his sight fixed, and his stride even, almost measured.

In a moment or two, he is at the periphery. Some of the Maidens rush to him, and he pauses to bend and embrace them. A hand comes here to touch a cheek, and another to embrace him about the mid-section, as those of his followers, too, are equally blessed and embraced. He is offered food and drink, but he declines it, and he turns to look at the edge of the horizon to adjudge the hour. Seemingly, he knows that there is time yet, so he turns and hands his staff to Eloise. And Rebecca comes forward to offer him an additional over-garment, which he also declines.

He walks into the midst of the crowd that is ever growing, and some fall to their knees. He touches a head in a blessing, and turns here and there to give a good word of cheer. Then he strides to Thaddeus, one of his followers, who extends his hands, and he removes his great over-garment, handing it to Thaddeus.

Again, Rebecca comes forward, her hands outstretched with a beautiful over-garment. As he looks into her eyes, he can see her intent, and we hear her speak these words: "Each one of us, all twelve, have placed our hands to this cloth. Each has woven into it our love and our truth. In the work which we all know lies ahead, wilt thou not honor us by wearing this, that we might be with you in this small way?"

His eyes soften as he looks now to see that the other Maidens have gathered to stand beside Rebecca, and he can see in each pair of eyes the special blessing that each bears in their heart. For a moment or two, his thoughts pass over the previous thirty years, the many teachings, the truths, the gifts, that these faithful Maidens have literally birthed into the Earth and gifted to him and others and to the Greatest of all.

He turns to focus his eyes upon Rebecca again, whose hands still hold out the silvery-gray garment, her fingertips kneading the edge of it as she holds it, outstretched in joyful intent. Without removing his gaze from her, he slowly bends one knee and then the other, to kneel before her.

His hands come up in the tradition of the Maidens' own gesture, and we hear him softly speak, audible only to these twelve: "The purity and sweetness of God's Spirit lives in the hearts of each of you. That which you have given to me, to the others, to the Master, I shall ever treasure, and my spirit shall embrace your gifts and you forever more. In the symbol of that which your hands have created, and in the power that each of you possesses, now woven into this garment, I give thanks. I shall wear this cloak, as I am permitted, unto the end. And so, as I receive the gift of your spirits, receive ye mine, as well, for we are one."

His head bows, and Rebecca steps forward, as do the others, to tenderly place the over-garment upon John's shoulders and body. Those who are gathered, seeing that John is kneeling, all fall to their knees. Some prostrate themselves in the tradition of the ancient teaching. The Maidens encircle him, and they, too, kneel.

And She steps forward to offer this prayer to Her sisters, and to this one, whose task is near completed.

"Our Father, Which art in Heaven, we hallow Thy name. In Thy Spirit's coming, so do we know the hope and promise is now to be fulfilled. Strengthen us evermore, that the path ahead can be followed with understanding, love, and compassion for all. Thou hast blessed me with the gift of opportunity eternal. So do I, in the presence of Thy sight, bless all those who have walked with me and shared in the great beauty and honor of this work."

As She continues Her prayer, She slowly walks about the circle of Maidens, who are facing inwards, towards John. She pauses, and her hand comes to rest upon the head of each of the Maidens, one by one. She speaks of them and the special uniqueness of each one, which they gifted to Her Son, and calls them by their spiritual name.

Our Lady, then, steps between the Maidens and into the circle to stand before John, who is kneeling, head bowed. She bends to place Her hand beneath his chin, uplifting his face that She might look upon him, Her son's playmate and friend. Her eyes and his meet, for they know they shall not gaze upon one another again in this lifetime.

John's hand comes up to touch the back of Hers, and She bends to kiss his forehead, and he, Her hand. Looking up then, John's face breaks into a great smile, and She reciprocates, Her hands going over Her heart.

Sprightly, John springs to his feet. "You are all blessed. You are all given the grace of God. Let us rejoice, that our God is a graceful God." And with a moment's final gaze upon Our Lady, and a turn about to gaze into the eyes of each of the Twelve, he offers the symbolic spiritual gesture. A hand goes over his heart, and he bows to them, turning swiftly to stride between them and down to the water's edge.

"Come! Let us be one with God. Let us join in oneness with eternity, for you are the children of God. Come! Let me awaken you," and he strides out into the water. He is followed a portion of the way by Thaddeus and several of the others, and they lead those who have gathered to him, one by one.

And so it goes. And the hour passes, and another. And the sun is now sufficient so as to illuminate the distant foothills.

Suddenly, all pause, for the song can be heard!

And He strides, equally so as did John, with a steady, measured pace, the morning breezes swirling His hair about His shoulders, and billowing His over-garment off to the side. Yet does He stride. And even though there is some distance, we can see that His face is warm and smiling.

John has turned, to his waist-section in the water. The others have stepped aside and formed a gentle semi-circle in the water, the center of which is John.

The Maidens, on the shore, have divided themselves and are kneeling to the right and left of what has now become a generous pathway leading to the water's edge. John's hand goes up in a greeting of one childhood friend to another, and instantly, the Master reciprocates, His smile broadening, their eyes fixed upon one another.

As He reaches the edge of the gathering, He turns, pausing

to stop before the first six Maidens on the left, touching a cheek, brushing a strand of hair back, touching a chin, leaning to place His forehead against theirs, calling them by their spiritual name, and He turns swiftly to do the same to the six on the right.

Whereupon, He comes to the center, where Our Lady stands a bit to the right. He extends His hands out, palms up, and She places Hers within His. They say not a word, but both smile and look upon one another, until She merely nods, placing Her hands again over Her bosom.

The Master turns, for a moment or two looking this way and that at the throngs of onlookers who press forward.

There are murmurs here and there...

"Is it He?"

"Do you think it is Him?"

"Why do they recognize Him?"

"Why do they salute Him?"

Slowly, He turns, and His eyes meet the Forerunner's. Without removing His eyes from John's, He strides steadily into the water and up to John. And there they stand, smiling.

It is John who raises his right hand and places it upon the Master's shoulder, and the Master, in turn, does the same to John.

"It begins, then," speaks John, softly.

The Master, smiling, nods, and slowly, they embrace. As they part, the Master speaks softly. "Thank you."

John merely nods, and reaches up to touch his beautiful new over-garment, glancing up over the Master's shoulder to see the eyes awide of the Maidens of Righteousness, and Our Lady's smiling face. She gives him a gentle nod, and he returns it to Her.

Stepping back a pace or so, John calls out in a loud voice, clearly, "Art Thou He, who has been sent of God?"

Only John can see the Master's great smile. And He answers softly, "I am."

The Master then comes unto John, and John receives Him with the sacred blessing of the Expectant Ones. When it is completed, the heavens illuminate. Then, as if through some mystical happenstance, a flock of beautiful doves circle about again and again, and one comes to land upon the Master's outstretched arm.

And John's firm voice can be heard, "Look you, one and all! This is the Son of God."

There are great outcries, and many fall to the ground. Many begin to beat upon their bodies and wail. Some commence psalm singing. Several run, shrieking, off into the wasteland beyond, for their hearts cannot perceive Him. Others who were nearby come, running to see who it is that this one of the wilderness has proclaimed to be the Son of God. A last glance from the Master, and the connection of their eyes communicates more than any words ever could.

John raises a hand, clenches it to a fist, and brings it to his heart. "Wherever Thou art, my spirit is with Thee."

The Master smiles, nods, and without a word turns and strides out of the water, up the gentle slope, and into His work.

CLOSING COMMENTS

Could it not be, dear friends, that thou art baptized in a similar way? That the simple ceremony we have offered to you above might be followed with this vision we have attempted in humbleness to recount to you? We shall, in those times ahead, so as our brother and sister in the Earth permit, offer you more about the beauty, the wonder, the joy that is a part of the way.

And some might ask, how is it that we might do so? Is it not against that which is aright in the eyes and teachings of so many? Is this not, in its essence and in its completeness, sacred and that which cannot be spoken?To those hearts and minds as would think these and other such thoughts, which might limit or preclude, which might cloud or mask or diminish, we can only offer this to you... If these fruits, as we offer them, are good, and if they inspire and bring goodness after their kind, then are they not, as the Master Himself has spoken, from a good tree? And if the tree is good and the tree is called the Tree of Life, then life itself ever offers the fruit of goodness.

But there must be those eyes which can see, and those hearts which are open to receive same. And if there is the con-tinuation of that which limits, occludes, blocks, minimizes, or denies the true gifts of God, then look to His words again. For we say to those who believe in such ways, thou hast heard Him not. It is He who has sent us. It is in His name that we give this, and that which shall be given in times ahead. But if you struggle against this, if you find something within self which cannot rejoice, as Our Lady Herself rejoices, then search this out. Look upon it. See from whence it has come, and how it has become an inhabitant of the temple of thy being.

The message is clear: He is ever with thee.

And if in these works we have served to, only one whit, bring His message to the forefront for you, then surely those who will follow will adjudge this to have been good.

As we leave you, let us offer you this one parting thought: What do you have to lose? Limitation? Fear? Some guilt? Any of these, and others, would you not gladly relinquish them? Then that is our invitation to you. Give them over, and pass beyond them. For as He, even as we speak, strides along the Path, having been proclaimed as He has, He gestures you to walk with Him. Might you not pray on this? For it is a good thought and a good prayer.

Our prayers and blessings are with you as merely an offer-ing. You may choose to accept or nay, for teachings of Truth do not bind, they do not confine nor limit. Teachings of Truth can be known to be Truth because they set you free.

6 - The Temptations of Christ

CHANNEL/AL MINER: The request for this reading is that I read Matthew 3:13 through 4:11 which I will do at this time:

Then cometh Jesus from Galilee to Jordan unto John, to be baptized of him.

But John forbade him, saying, I have need to be baptized of thee, and comest thou to me?

And Jesus answering said unto him, Suffer it to be so now: for thus it becometh us to fulfill all righteousness. Then he suffered him.

And Jesus, when he was baptized, went up straightway out of the water: and, lo, the heavens were opened unto him, and he saw the Spirit of God descending like a dove, and lighting upon him:

And lo a voice from heaven, saying, This is my beloved Son, in whom I am well pleased.

Then was Jesus led up of the spirit into the wilderness to be tempted of the devil.

And when he had fasted forty days and forty nights, he was afterward an hungered.

And when the tempter came to him, he said, If thou be the Son of God, command that these stones be made bread.

But he answered and said, It is written, Man shall not live by bread alone, but by every word that proceedeth out of the mouth of God.

Then the devil taketh him up into the holy city, and setteth him on a pinnacle of the temple,

And saith unto him, If thou be the Son of God, cast thyself down: for it is written, He shall give his angels charge con-

cerning thee: and in their hands they shall bear thee up, lest at any time thou dash thy foot against a stone.

And Jesus said unto him, It is written again, Thou shalt not tempt the Lord thy God.

Again, the devil taketh him up into an exceeding high mountain, and sheweth him all the kingdoms of the world, and the glory of them;

And saith unto him, All these things will I give thee, if thou wilt fall down and worship me.

Then saith Jesus unto him, Get thee hence, Satan: for it is written, Thou shalt worship the Lord thy God, and him only shall thou serve.

Then the devil leaveth him, and, behold, angels came and ministered unto him. Amen. \

SPONSOR'S QUESTION

Lama Sing, would you please give us commentary from your viewpoint on the physical, mental, emotional, and spiritual lessons contained in this story of the baptism and temptations of Jesus.

LAMA SING COMMENTARY

There is a crispness in the air, and yet the warmth from the sun seems to penetrate and remove this. There is the clarity and the sparkle of the water as these gently pass by John, who is standing not quite mid stream, peering a bit into the distance, in a sense of expectation, wonder, and love.

The light which cometh in that distance is sufficient so as to even part the grouping standing before John, previously listening to his prayers and his teachings, as, with confidence and surety, the figure strides unto the water's edge.

For these are as brothers, come to meet one another during the course of their individual and group destiny.

THE LESSONS

We shall not repeat nor further describe here, but rather we shall turn from this moment to the moment of the Master's emergence, wherein the light of heaven transcended and shone upon the Master and, as well, John. And wherein it was heard to be spoken from the very heavens themselves those words and more, as ye have them recorded.

The Baptism

We find that the purpose of the baptism is to acknowledge, in essence, the acceptance of a certain pathway: that each entity has, in their experiences, some form, some expression, some experience, wherein they shall meet that force which strives ever to assist them and purify them.

The Purifier

When this decision is made, in and of the will of self, then the Purifier is present and cometh forth to do that work with thee. As thou art anointed, then, there must come the tempering of that steel which has been forged, and by the thrusting of a forged implement into the coolness of water, one finds that its strength is made lasting. And it is thusly tempered, that its spirit will endure any labors to which it might be placed.

Then that brief description tells all. For as Jesus emerged and was made pure (in the sense of His affirmation and the unification of those forces borne through the Baptist and borne through the will of the Master in Jesus), there was the merging of the spirit of the Christ into the man, Jesus. This was the final stage of initiation, the final purification process, and thus, the emerging of that which is the living and eternal example, that which unified the light from the kingdom of God to ever walk the Earth wherever the spirit of man shall call out upon the Christ. We find in this, there has been prepared the way for all who would willingly follow. Be not misled by words, by titles, or names, for it is the Spirit which is borne in man which holds the potential; in the physical, the body was purified.

The Tempering

The fast commenced. We have purged with the mental. We have purged with that force spiritual, through the teachings given by the Essenes, through the temples of wisdom, and in the greatest of all temples, in the western lands of the Master's own homeland. We come into this time where the anointment was bound unto the man as a light. For the force of God was brought to the fore from within the man by ascending the steps of consciousness, by illuminating the chakras, by building acceptance, by using grace and karma and the Universal Law. All of these did bring the man Jesus unto becoming the Christ.

Then what of this purging of the body? If the man is in that sense (as implied above) perfect, what need to purge the body? Does not one prepare the soil, even so, when the seed is strong? Does not even the good shepherd find the easiest pathway for their flock? Is there not even in each vessel one who commands and directs, lest that vessel be lost at sea? Then there is one force, spiritual, and the body must be made unto it, in harmony and obedient.

Though, ye ask, "What of fasting? This, then, weakening the body, building hunger, desire, and thirst?" This, then, is the curing, the purifying, the tempering, of the spirit, which was forged in the river by the Baptist; and more, of course, for the life itself and the incarnations preceding, these are all the forging, the shaping, and the fashioning. But as the energy is balanced by building a dependence upon the will, the spirit within, as the body is sublimated to an extent and its dependence upon the external for its sustenance, for its endurance, is diminished, there remains only that entity in the mental and in the spiritual form. The temple is swept clean, and there resides, then, that which is to be, by its nature, tempered.

Then the Tempter

Then enter the Tempter and the force which is to build the eternal strength into this light. Is there not want when one is hungered? In the isolation of the fast and in the wilderness, there are none to encourage nor support. There can be a wilderness for thee, dear friends, even in the midst of a great grouping or gathering of peoples, for the wilderness may be that of spirit and not of companionship of the physical form. Jesus stated clearly His hunger, and more. Yet He sought not from the Earth but from God, knowing even then and more that this is the eternal nourishment. So the teaching is to sustain the body first, by that which is the Law, the Word of God. For that is the way to truly nourish and grow. That is the pathway which can lead to an eternal fulfillment of any need, any want.

There was the encouragement here, to each of you, that God provides all that is needed. If ye will remove all other forces (just as given in the literal, the written word, and in the spiritual force which comes with it), remove all other illusions or forces that could be interpreted to be contributing, strip self of all possible other sources and find that, when the will (that is, the mind and the spirit) are forged into oneness, the body will endure and will be sustained. The purging of the body opens the centers and provides for the flow of light. It provides for the meaning to life, knowing that, so as one walks upon the Earth, there can be naught in the Earth which can live that is eternal. Only by the reactions of thee, each one, can you find true Light and lasting or eternal fulfillment of your needs.

There is that force or side of self which seeks ever to build, and that force which seeks to break down or to destroy. There is that force which goes beyond self and reaches into the eternal, and there is that force which attempts to cling to that which is the present, the illusion, and is reluctant to grow or progress. Then there is the tempting here of the spirit, the mind, and the body, the testing of the will, the testing of the faith, and the testing, indeed, of all of these in the point of intersect with the Earth, which is the body physical.

Bargaining with God

To be carried to a higher place is to be carried to a perspective, a point of view, an understanding, a wisdom, a pinnacle, if you will, in the midst of thy brethren. Symbolically, this permits you to control, because if all is known or can be seen, is there not infinite control simply in the knowledge of that which shall transpire?

In one aspect, this is how the kingdom of the Earth was offered unto the Master and rejected. In the spiritual sense, the Master was offered a place before God, rather than as His Son. He was offered the position that He would become one apart from God to be worshipped, to be respected, in the sense as one directs their respect and worship unto God.

The force that the Master was requested to honor was this: that force which seeks to build itself as an individual apart from God. Not a demonic force, not a force of an individual, an alter- or anti-deity called Satan, but rather the force of darkness which is the illusion of one's own potential grandeur and one's own potential apartness from God.

In the instance, as written above, were Jesus to cast Himself downwards, would He have perished? Would His body have been crushed beneath? Would the Angelic Host have appeared to gather Him up softly and gently, and return Him unto that lofty position from whence He may have left? We think not, for to have done so would have presented a tool, an implement in the service of God that would be, thusly, less than perfect. The Master Himself would have willed the conclusion of that incarnation rather than to go forward imperfect, knowing that this imperfection, even though it may have appeared slight, would have been sufficient to have limited the works which He was offered to do for His Father.

Could He not have accepted this challenge and, while proving that He was, in essence, protected, established that He, indeed, was the Son of God? Would any of you have believed it because of this action? Do you believe in the present because of His other actions? Do you believe because of His healing works that He, indeed, was the Son of God? Be mindful of thy answer, for if you affirm this, then you also affirm that He has told you that these things and even more shall each of ye do!

Breads of Temptation

What bread, then, was sought by the forces of darkness to tempt the Master with? The bread of Earth? The bread of eternal life and joy? What bread, then, art thou tempted with? The bread of doubt? The bread of reason and logic? What is the pinnacle from whence thee would have self thrown, or even moreso, that thee would choose to jump from? Do thee tempt God in any wise in asking that He do this or that work for thee or for another? And when it shall, perhaps, come to pass that thou dost not see this work done, that a doubt is born?

But if there is that work wherein the need is great, and wherein that entity or entities whom are seeking have, indeed, relinquished their doubt and believe unto that work which ye might do in His name, can thee do less than respond to this? Then the teaching here is, of course, the Word of God which is the Law, and this is the nourishment to the spirit. And the spirit becomes at one with God. The mind seeks through the spirit, and through this seeking, forms a bond, a channel that, then, by its nature, can nourish the body. It is the manna. It is the bread of life. It is the eternal sustenance. Ye would ask, many of thee: Where is this? I have oft been in joyous prayer. I have often fasted and meditated, and yet naught appeared for me. Nothing came. I was given naught, and I yet seek.

But is it true, dear friends, that the seeking, the fasting, and the purposes for same were the same as this, given? The same as the example of the man Jesus? Go forward in the story, the tale, and the factual account, as they are all combined here in the life of the man Jesus.

KNOWING AND APPLYING

He did not deny this or that, but accepted that which was present in the Earth as that which is proper in a realm wherein He walked as the Son of God and the son of man. He affirmed, in the examples of the purification, that these things are the way to think, these attitudes are the way to direct the activity of life:

Attitudes to Hold

- To not accept that ye must mount a great high place and be tempted to test yourselves.

- That ye must not call upon self alone for the source, the sustenance, of your very life's joy; but to seek this nourishment, as well, from God.

- And further, to seek not thy reward or the merit of thy labors by the measure of the Earth, in the material, the physical, or that which is the recognition, as a title or what not; but rather, seek in the fashioning of an attitude which states, I need these not, these that are known to be limiting factors; I need only the sense within self of knowing that my intent has been pure and my way is good, because the pattern is that which I believe in the very most within.

Every Experience Strengthens

In the Bread of Life, there is not that which is in Earth that can better nourish the spiritual force; there is nothing in the Earth that is a food for the spirit. Yet every experience in the Earth builds and strengthens the spirit. But it is neither of the grain nor the fibers of plants nor that of the flesh of any beastie; it is by the sharing and exchange of experience with thy brethren. It is out of the love and compassionate understanding that is builded through these relationships, that thee find thy true sustenance.

Yes, there are those among thee in the Earth [realm] who might debate this matter with us here, humbly, stating that without sustaining the body, it will surely perish. Then to this we answer, give unto that, that which is proper for the realm of its existence.

In the body physical, build that nourishment which is of the physical. In the body mental, build that which is of its own nature. In the body spiritual, build that which is of God's Word, for that forms the pattern which makes possible all of the former. See?

THE WORD OF GOD

There is within each of you all of that given above. If ye are seeking, ye will be guided. If you seek the purification, then the Baptist will appear unto you. If you seek to know the Law, then a teacher will respond and give it unto thee. But if thee seek to find the joy and eternal nature of Consciousness, then only in God's Laws, His Word, can these be understood and thusly obtained.

Experiencing the Forces

The Word of God, then, is the lesson which becomes real and lasting when you experience and accept and understand same. These are oft-times referred to as the Laws Universal. They are as the spoken Word of God. These are that Force which has made the fabric of your very existence. These are the thought of God, which made perfection and the harmony of all vibration. These are those Forces that are God Himself. And thee must experience them in order that thee know them and accept them in every aspect, in every potential realm, in every possible manifestation that these might make. Whether the smallest grain of sand on the furthest beach or seashore distant from thee, or the greatest celestial sphere in the heavens beyond thy perception, each of these must be known, just as the heart and need of the brethren closest and most distant to thee must, as well, be known.

Understanding Karma

If thee do not respond to the need of another, art thou damned? Likely so, for self will judge, based upon the Law. Is this the damnation spoken of by so many? No, it is not! By choosing to judge self, you create the opportunity for karma to take place. This is merely the opportunity to experience again some event, some activity that shall allow for the understanding to create grace. It is the Grace, then, that is the bread of our Father's Word, and it is that of which thee will nourish self and emerge pure. It is not the lot of man to continually be persecuted by some force unseen, to continually be tempted and lured by some apparent opposing force. These are all Forces of God.

Appreciating the Paradox

The opposing Force is that which is against God because it knows God not in its consciousness. It knows only of itself and the desires of self. It is this Force that asks thee to hurl self from the pinnacle, to use the power of God and eternal wisdom and knowledge, to command thy brethren and the Earth and other realms, and to feed self through those Forces unseen. And yet those Forces are the very Forces that, if used, may very often cause a limitation. It is, in essence, that as self struggles to emerge as a Child of God, there is the paradox.

In the paradox, then, understand that man is given, as an entity and as an extension of the life force or soul of same, that which they are worthy to bear, that to which they have the strength to labor. To give unto man more than this, would be as to present them the kingdom of the Earth. There would begin, perhaps, a great mental, spiritual, and emotional struggle to determine how to properly and wisely control and direct same. For there would not be the evolvement of that man, that entity, unto the awareness sufficiently so as to allow the flow of God to do the commanding and to ascend into that consciousness, to assume the rightful position with God.

Divine in Intent

Those stones, had they been turned into loaves of bread (as surely they may have been done; hast thou not witnessed the fishes and loaves), then what would be their nourishment? Who would these have imparted a sustenance to? For it was not Jesus who asked of them, who sought them, but the alter-force, that which is called the Devil, or its like… the Tester. So it is to not succumb to that which is idle, to not use that which is thy divine nature to fulfill that which is not divine in its intent and in its ultimate good; but to use that as is thine own eternal nature where there is the need, and to open self to know the difference and to feel and be guided.

All of these teachings do not mean, dear friends, that ye

will not have joyous experiences which will often seem irrelevant, not truly spiritual, at times even humorous. But think thee not that these are not proper for thee, for these are the joyous blessings of a loving Father and His willing workers seeking to encourage, to enlighten, to bring a sense of love and laughter and gaiety unto the experience of growth. For the growth is not intended to be one of an intense purification, but rather, to gently, to lovingly, apply the Law of Grace and to allow this grace to transcend the need for the actual experiencing and to quickly, easily, and beautifully build understanding.

CLOSING COMMENTS

And so as we prepare to conclude here, we state again, there is much that is not written which took place regarding all of this. In the present, for reasons that cannot be stated, this cannot be totally given. This much do we give: The Master, Jesus, had no real need, in the sense of the Earth plane, to go unto John if He was the Master. Thusly, thee must know that He did so for reasons that are beyond the Earth and beyond the physical and perhaps beyond the logic of your minds. Neither did John have the need to perform the action of baptizing Jesus, for he had only to speak the words and it would be so, just as it was with Jesus, for they were brothers of spirit.

KEYS TO THINE OWN BAPTISM

This was done, all of these things and more, that thee would know them ever to be as keys unto the baptism of thine own spirit, and as answers unto the testings of thine own will in the Earth and all realms. The subsequent experiences in the lives of both of these entities and the others were so as to show you other keys, other teachings, initiations, which are all a part of that opportunity for thee to become the teacher, the servant, a leader and a follower, and both of a good shepherd and the gentle lamb. But above all, these were done to help thee to realize that thou art all Children of God, and that as thou art willing, it is given unto thee.

7 - *Jesus Heals - Part 1*

CHANNEL/AL MINER: This is a request for a topical research reading dealing with the healings as performed by Jesus. I would like to thank the sponsors for their well thought-out questions and, of course, for the beautiful and inspiring topic.

SPONSOR'S QUESTIONS

Dear Lama Sing, Here are the stories of three healings by Jesus. Please use these to illustrate how Jesus healed people, and how we might heal people also.

1. In the story of the woman with an issue of blood, please comment particularly on Jesus' feeling that the power had gone forth from Him. This implies that He contained His power like a reservoir, and was aware when some was drained out. Perhaps this relates to His statement, *I am the Way,* which implies that His etheric energy, His aura, His beingness, is important. Perhaps the energy around each of us is important. Perhaps when it is perfected we, too, can become a way or the way. Please also discuss Jesus' seeming temporary difficulty identifying the woman in the crowd after her healing. (And for reference, that can be found in Mark, Chapter 5, verses 25 - 34.)

2. In the story of the man born blind, did He enter the Earth knowing that Jesus would come along and heal him? In this healing, Jesus uses clay, spittle, and washing to effect the transformation of the body. Why does He sometimes use "devices" like these, and sometimes not? (This can be found in John, Chapter 9, verses 1-17, for those of you who would like to refresh your memory.)

3. In the story of the man at Bethesda, it seems as if the pool was a healing place. Please comment on healing places in the Earth. How do they work? Do they provide a passage of pure spiritual energy somehow, and become an Earthly form of

the way? (And the story of the man at Bethesda is found in John, Chapter 5, verses 1-15.)

4. These last two stories also bring up the issue of healing on the Sabbath. Is there an esoteric meaning behind the arguments between Jesus and the Pharisees about healing on the Sabbath?

5. Please comment on Jesus' instructions to people to "sin no more." Were these sins errors of thought? Of emotion? Of body? Of spirit? Did people immediately understand what He meant for them?

As in all these stories, there are undoubtedly subtleties that we don't understand. Please feel free to discuss these and any other topics that you judge to be important or of interest to us.

Thank you, and blessings.

LAMA SING COMMENTARY

There are, of course, many parallels and truths that can be found in the works and teachings of the Master. And there are as many of those who have served Him, who yet bear this message in His name in the Earth [realm], and in realms near and far. As you listen to that which we shall offer in humbleness, consider that within you there may well be, as has been mentioned above in the questions and suggestions, the Way.

TOUCHING THE HEM

In the midst of that throng, as the Master walked, there was the continual pressing, the calling out, the reaching unto Him. Some reached and grasped His sleeve as He went by. The Disciples sought with vigor and growing frustration to protect and preserve the Master, some space about Him as He proceeded. Yet, He was, as ever, untroubled, ever at peace and joyful, smiling, touching, and speaking as He walked.

In that moment when this woman came to Him, with such a faith that she believed in all of her being that, here is the Light of the Earth, here is the Son of God; believing that, as she might touch but the hem of His garment, she would be healed. And so she did, and was healed.

Faith Flowed from and to Jesus

What do you discern here that is unique? Even the faithful Disciples who were with the Master spoke to Him, "Goodness, Lord, how could you ask 'Who has touched me?' Everyone is touching you, or trying." What was the distinct essence that made for the connection, that made the way passable for her faith to be fulfilled? We just spoke it: her faith.

Instantly, the Master knew and felt the flow of God's presence and Spirit within and about Him, flowing (channeling if you will) to the faithful woman. As He turned about and proclaimed, "Who has touched me?" it was not so much that He knew not in the sense of being able to discern her from the grouping, for in a moment or two He could have easily so done. It was, rather, a part of the healing process and the wisdom of the Master as He called out.

She Made the Way Passable

Of course, as you read of this, you will see that the woman was troubled, feeling indeed that she had taken that not of her right, for there were so many in need who were seeking. So she came before the Master and threw herself at His feet. That very action was the completion of her healing work. When she proclaimed her faith to the Master, she proclaimed it to herself. She is the one who made the way passable. The Master is the cup from which she drank.

It is true that there is a certain reservoir, as you have defined it, an energy, a field oft referred to as the auric field or aura. It is this peripheral boundary of the field of energy, which is self, that is governed by and (as you claim it) protected through Universal Law. This is the field or definition of your uniqueness. You can, with abandon, fill this envelopment as you would. It is your choice: to walk about in this *sphere* (if you will), filled with light; or you can open it and let the thoughts around you, the energies and influences around you, enter in. You can do this to the extent that you claim them and they become resident within this sphere of light around you; or you can do so only to the extent that you are assessing and becoming aware of what is around you and not claiming it, merely acknowledging its presence and sustaining your individual dominion, joy, and healing grace.

Connection Enables Detection of the Flow

The Master's connection with God is complete. Therefore, it is not so much that this exemplifies a depletion of the energy or virtue of the Master, though, curiously, some have written it in this way, but is rather that He could detect the flow of this through Him. This is different than Him intentionally choosing someone to reach out and touch, imparting a gift or a blessing or offering healing energy. So it was that this was not by His initial intent, not a decision from Him. Yet, of course, the woman's faith opened and made passable a pathway of light (if you will) between the Master and she, that path literally being her faith. Again and again, you will see this was the Master's test more oft than not, with the exception of those which were the fulfilling of the prophecies, which He also honored.

As each of you consider yourselves, as is written, the golden cup, the golden chalice, the vessel in which the Spirit of God resides, then, by opening self to that which is eternal, so do you keep this ever replenished, that thereafter you can never deplete it, for it is always replaced as it is given. Testing, believing, knowing, claiming, living, being, all of these things are facets of what you are seeking.

THE BLIND MAN

In those instances where the Master, as exemplified with the blind man, came about certain works and knew them to be purposeful. He knew this. As we have given previously, He is one with the Universal Forces – Universal Consciousness and of course God, that are really not separate but demarcated here for understanding.

Who Bears the Sin

Thus, when questioned, "Who bears the sin of this man's dis-ease or infirmity?" and He answered, "None such as ye have stated, but rather that our Father's works might be done and be known," because the man had (as in the previous example) not come forward in the same manner, with the utterness of his faith, and yet came forward seeking, the Master gave of the Earth to the Earth (in a manner of speaking). For it is not this man's faith which has healed him, but rather that the Law shall be shown and demonstrated to be perfect, and that "I am the Son of God, through which God doeth the work."

Giving Opportunity to Demonstrate Faith

To take that which is of the Earth to heal and/or cleanse or purify that which is in the Earth is a Universal Truth. It is to demonstrate that, in the Earth is the Spirit of God, with the fullness of God's potential in everything, as we have given it in our prayer at the onset. So as He, with spittle, made a covering and placed it on the man's eyes, He then gave him the opportunity to demonstrate faith. Though he came forth not with those words, but a desire only in his heart, he did demonstrate his faith by doing precisely what the Master said he should do. When he washed away the earth, he washed away the limitation, for both are in the Earth plane: one is darkness, and the other is light. They are of the same Creator. So the Law is perfect and whole. The man, through his demonstration of faith in the Master, followed His word. So was he healed.

All Is of God

It is for you to know by this example that in all things the Spirit of God is present, whether this be an herb, a bit of clay and spittle, a mark of some sort made with ash, a medicine which is the derivation of those who have dedicated themselves and are, after all, also Children of God. And those who, through their dedication and skills, can perform surgical work upon the body, there is naught in that surgery room that isn't of God.

The empowerment of self to be a channel of blessings is to know these things, and to see them and to claim them, and to support them on a foundation eternally of faith, a faith that begins within. The Master chose that which was equal to the need, equal to that of those who were seeking. Whether that is to answer the call of one who comes with utter, absolute faith, or to take and give to one to fulfill the prophecy and to demonstrate the Law and the omnipotence of God and God's Spirit in all things, or to exemplify the Way.

I Am the Way

He also stated, "This is the way." But His claiming, "I am the Way" is a statement of empowerment. Notice all throughout that the Master freely spoke these words when He knew His ministry had begun. And in this, He knew that those who could see and hear would understand that He did this by way of example, having attained and claimed same, that we would know He is the Way, and that this is within us, as well.

When one challenges the shadows of the valley that is called Earth, there are those forces which will ever strive to resist. Even unto the Master did they oft-times plead with Him. And to you, and to those who might come unto you, they could, perhaps, be more forthright, or more devious, more subtle. Is not habit, indeed, a shadowy force if it limits you? Yet, there are habits which are of the light, and which free you.

Again, it is the presence of your thought, your spirit, and your choices within same that surround you with the aura of faith, that nothing can reside, nor would it seek to, where there is light, unless that thing is Light. But that which is the shadow upon the Earth and in it, coming to you, must know itself for what it is. For if you bear the Light, then it will know itself to be a shadow. But if there are none who know and bear the Light, how can the shadows know themselves?

There is a great truth here; it is our prayer that you shall hear it. And so, we offer it again in this way:

Earth: The Valley of Opportunity of Contrasts

We have used the words valley and the valley of the shadows in relevance to the Earth. We do not mean to imply that the Earth is bad, that the Earth is a place, singularly, of darkness; neither do we wish to infer that these are not present, for they are. Most all know this. The Earth is that valley of opportunity in which the contrasts are evident. And yet, the dominant force is so often that of tradition and habit, the familiar, rather than the willingness to go forth and claim, often alone.

Greater Things Shall Ye Do

Is it not, then, knowing this, that, by your very presence and having claimed His Light, that you, by taking this Light and being joyful in it and giving of it – isn't it true, mustn't it be true – that if you are doing things of this nature in the Earth, you are, in fact, doing what the Master said you would do? For the shadows are not without their essence. Some live in the houses called bodies and minds of others about you in the Earth. Your light is an offering of healing grace, and the Christ Light within you is the gift you are bearing.

Remember, "All these and greater things shall ye do." You do them, so many of you, so often, and you know it not. Now it is our prayer that you will acknowledge this, know it, and claim it. Look to the Master as thy guide. He claimed, He acknowledged, He spoke forthrightly. Even more importantly, He was the living example of His own truth and teaching.

HEALING ON THE SABBATH

The designation of the Sabbath is the designation of the seventh center, the crown chakra. It is a part of the mysticism of the Kabala and other similar teachings, and in this teaching there is great truth. That we might rise up upon the previous centers, as the first six of seven golden steps, and, coming to the seventh, therein would we rest.

Yet, they knew it not but only by the letter of the law, not by its spirit. And yet, the Master was the spirit of the Law, is the spirit of the Law, and ever shall be, and this same is within you. So as they criticized, chastised, and sought to bring revulsion and such against the Master for doing works on the Sabbath, so were they, in their own spirits, denying their right to reach this highest level in Earth [consciousness]. They wore the garb and the signets of office, of high spiritual standing and judgment, and yet, they, in their stature and in the fullness of their own importance, could see not.

Claiming, Living, Acting

So it could be clearly said that the Master did these works not apart from the law, but within it; not to dishonor the Sabbath and its meaning of reverence to God, but herein, above all else, to honor it. While others were idle, and perhaps righteously so, the Master was claiming and living and acting.

As those came to Him, just as they might come to you, dear friends, they didn't ask of Him, "I know today is the Sabbath, so could I have an appointment for you to heal me on the morrow? Could I meet you at such and such a place when it is according to the law, and would you then heal me?" Of course, the absurdity and humor of this is intentional. The point of this is not so much so that we are attempting to criticize or judge even the Pharisees. While there is good measure here upon which to judge, we do not.

Living the Spirit of the Law

The point of this is, the Master demonstrated, here again, to those who saw themselves as the law, that their interpretation and their judgment, and their judgment of those who violated the law must never be, never upon its letter, but upon its living spirit.

"I am the Light and the Way. The Father is within me, and I within Him. We are one. Believe unto me, and you shall be made whole. Eternal life shall be yours."

"Blasphemy!" they cried. And yet, He loved them. So much so that He was willing to teach them, as well. As He said,

"The Father doeth the work," then are they to chastise God for working on His holy day? Where does this circle of their truth begin and end? Does it begin with their purpose? Or the belief in their heart? Have they come to their station in life through study, through memorization of the words, the capacity to recite at will from the holy writ?

Here is a simple man born into obscurity, prophesied in His coming, whose tenure, although brief, lives throughout eternity, knowing the Law, living it. The greatest of all these, in terms of steps or conditions, was His living of the Law. He challenged the Pharisees on their own terms, in their own dominion, under their noses.

Does He not also, lovingly, challenge each and every one of us? Aren't His words still within you as you heard them in those times and hear them again now? All these things – not some of them, not those which you are fond of, all of them – and greater shall ye do: the promise of hope, a recognition of your oneness with Him.

Healing Places, Holy Places

In the spirit of the Earth itself, as recognized as that Spirit of the Living God, there are anomalies, holy places, places where, as you call them, energies come together and form, literally, founts of light or fountains of water. There are, indeed, just so many of these. Some are stationary, some are not, some are borne about the face of the Earth in the hands and hearts of the faithful. You could be one of these, right now, one step away from claiming same.

Empowering Self as a Fount of Blessing

There are those who have the awareness and the faith and the righteousness within to empower themselves in differing ways and in diverse places. There have been those times in past, and are in present, where such have the capacity to call upon the Forces of God to bring forth that which could be called the making of the Way; perhaps, on a scale small and local, but according to Universal Law, these know their righteousness. And for reasons of their own guidance and knowledge, have and do bless places, people, and things.

The Spirit of God Is the Substance

So it was that several of the great prophets, and the Forerunner, and others, did bless this pool. At first, a simple pool by a simple gate to the city. And as entities did come unto this, and those whose faith made the way passable for them to be healed, so was it given to them. From that, then of course there followed, as might be expected, the belief, the faith, in the pool's healing potential. And which is it that nourishes, if not like unto like? So as there was the imparting of what could be called the healing grace and the bringing together of the anomalies, in the sense of the more technical in the Earth, so did the faith of those who went unto this pool, seeking, further empower it.

Is holy water more holy because it is here, in this container, where it has been blessed? Or is it equally holy to the dying entity in a desert who is handed the same water in a cup? You must judge this for yourself. And it is and ever shall be your faith which shall make you whole. The Christ is within all things as a potential. The Spirit of God is the substance of existence itself. You are His Child. Shall He do less for thee than another? Which are the keys here? Those of truth and simplicity, or those of the convoluted folds of the shadows so readily found in the Earth?

Judgment is not wrong. It is good, and has righteousness about it. You must judge, lest you cannot tell the path of light from the path of shadows, knowing the difference, and being able to grow from the understanding of those differences, is one of the wondrous gifts that the Earth offers.

Darkness is not evil, it is an intended contrast; man and woman are not different, they are complementary. Joy comes on the morrow, so it is written. And yet, where does it come from? Has it been dispatched from some distant location, celestially, and we are awaiting its arrival? Must the Master enter on a cloud of light for you to claim Him?

"I am ever with thee." He said this. The choice is simple, as truth so often is. You can believe, or nay. All too often, the shadow is alluring, because it is familiar, because it is known. There is a certain degree of comfort in that which is known. There is a certain degree of apprehension, and perhaps even fear for some, in the unknown.

Demonstration of Faith

The man spoke to Jesus from his heart, and the Master knew, for He could see the man's spirit. He knew instantly all that He would [need] to know about him; this was always delivered to the Master instantly. Yet, not in the sense as you would think, coming from afar in the outstretched hands of some angelic being, even though these are ever with Him, then as now; but because He is one with God. Universal Consciousness is God. Universal Consciousness is the All. Even this man at Bethesda is a part of the Universal Consciousness.

What a small matter, then, for the Master to look into the man and see him, feel him, know him, and the man's dis-ease, so long borne. He did not curse those who went before him. Even though he had awaited patiently his turn, his opportunity, to enter the healing water, yet he stood and stood and waited and waited. And as the Master came before him and asked of him, the man demonstrated his faith. He also demonstrated other qualities self-evident in that which we have given. But what is the single outstanding, even though not readily self-evident as in other works, that the Master could see and know to be good the man's loving patience and lack of anger, the fortitude with which these thirty-eight years he had borne this dis-ease? These are truths. But the greatest of all is this man's faith.

And so our Lord saw it, knew it, and commanded him to take up his bed and walk. The man heard this, not only with ear but in that same state of faith which he had builded up in his tenure here, at this gate of the pool to Bethesda. And so he did harken unto his own spirit, and he was healed. Here again, this entity was challenged, as the blind man was. Some even so as to say, "You are not that one who was before. You are a different one." To which he would answer, "No, it is I. I am he. I am the same."

THE HEART OF THE PHARISEE

Come with us for just a moment, dear friends. Let us visit the heart of the Pharisees. Their way of life through childhood was dictated unto them. Their ability to express their joy, their love, their laughter, was given only narrow berth to be expressed. They were continually mandated to as to *this is righteous, this is not; this is holy, and this is evil.*

In short, their lives leading up to this, the culmination of their position in this state of authority, was as rigid as the reed through which the water flows. It could not divert itself from the imposed channel in which it had grown. All that they were, all that they knew, all that they loved, was represented in their stature and their accomplishment in life. How could they know and live the spirit of the law, when they had never been offered that as an opportunity?

Sowing Seeds into Darkness

This is likened unto a farmer planting his seeds in a great box, and then placing a cover on it and putting it away, coming back at the end of the season, and questioning, "Why are there no fruits to harvest from these seeds?" We would do well, all, to ask ourselves, "Have we sown any of our seeds into darkness? Have we placed them into containers, closed those, and put them deep within our heart or spirit?"

Imagine these entities, upon hearing of someone walking about, casually healing people, and doing so in the name of God. That certainly would lure them out of the channel of their rigid upbringing. It certainly would challenge their stature, all that they knew to do, all they knew to teach, and their judgments, based upon the letter of the law.

Cleaving unto the Letter, Ignoring the Spirit

Have you certain laws within you to which you cleave unto the letter and ignore the spirit? Are you channeling that Child within you along a narrow, confined passageway? Or are you encouraging it to dance upon the meadows of life in the midst of the myriad of God's flowers thereupon, singing His songs of praise and joy, claiming, loving, being?

Remember the parable the Master gave of separating the wheat from the chaff, and that some seeds fall upon hard ground or stone and bear not fruit after their kind? The good farmer tills the earth, nurtures it, sows the seeds with love, feeds those seeds with water and unto their need, and his harvest is abundant. The Pharisees are not good farmers, not because they intend it so, but because they know it not. So, when the blind man, now seeing, came before them, could they do different? Some did. Some heard, in spite of the rigidity in which they lived.

ALL THINGS ARE POSSIBLE WHEN YOU BELIEVE

When one comes before you, who could not see and now does, when one who has been dis-eased and your prayer has been as a commandment of God – good fellow, good woman, take up thy bed, arise, and walk, thou art healed – when that knowledge comes unto you, shall you be as the Pharisee, or good farmer? The Pharisee denies the harvest, for he knows it not; the farmer expects the harvest, and he gathers it with love and gratitude, and sows it, a portion of same, again and again. Truth is also joyful, as well as simple. You are truth. You are His light. When you believe unto yourself, all things are possible, first, for you.

The woman's issue before she touched the Master's garment was spoken to by many, and yet she was not healed. When all was gone, all of her means and all the possibilities for her to be healed, she had naught to believe upon, except that within her. So she came to the Master, having exhausted all other means and all of her material goods in the process.

How great is one's faith, when there is nowhere else to turn? How wonderful is God, when there are no other hands outstretched to help thee? How wonderful are those who can have abundance, and yet claim, as this woman did, who had naught? For they know truth. God is abundance and health and joy and service and love; you are His Child.

CLOSING COMMENTS

The message in all of this, as we have intended to give it above, is the same message that some of you literally heard two thousand years ago, approximate. We have only brought these words and thought-forms from the Master Himself forward to you. We have presented them before you in humbleness before the Master Himself in this work.

The Master loves you. The Master is at your side. Who do you love? At whose side dost thou stand?

"I am the Light and the Way. It is through me that you shall come to oneness with God." So very simple, beautiful, and clear: the I AM is within you, even as we speak. Even as He promised it, "I AM ever with you."

8 - *The Beatitudes*

LAMA SING COMMENTARY

It is a warm, pleasant surrounding. There are hills and mountains about, and there is the ever-changing hue of the green and slightly bluish tint to the grasses dotted with wild flowers. The peoples are moving from all directions, gathering in this gentle valley, which slopes slightly upwards to a mount.

Behind, as we turn, we can see the sea as it stretches out to touch and to hold the horizon. The sounds, the odors, of the water carried upon a gentle, perfumed breeze. Each individual flower seems to radiate its colors and burst them forth in a symphony of loving color.

There are entities before us of every age, every manner, and from many different lands, and among this multitude, hundreds whom this day have received blessings from the Master, the Christ. There is an air of joyous expectation.

As we turn our gaze to the summit, the mount, a beautiful blue sky comes into our focus, quite abundantly filled with immense, billowing white clouds, and through the clouds, patches of blue can be perceived. A cloud begins to enlighten with golds, yellows, reds, and it parts as though a bursting beam of light from the sun or from the heavens has struggled to reach forth and touch the Master, upon the mount.

There, we can see that He has chosen a spot to rest where-in a shepherd has a small flock. Several of the lambs of the flock have come to rest at His feet. And there, the dove, which ever seems to follow the Master, appears in the beam of sun-light and floats downwards to rest upon His shoulder. Those who follow with the Master are gathered near at hand. They are among the grouping of those the Master has sent forth to many lands who are, as well, gathered here now.

The Master has a wish to leave His virtue with each of thee. He has the love and the desire to give to thee that knowledge which thou might carry throughout eternity, as the Father touches and unites with the Master.

All who are guided across the entire valley and upwards to the slopes of the gentle inclines, resting among the flowers and grasses, warm in the radiance which now seems to fill the entire area each one can see the Master clearly as though He were at hand's breadth from them, and can hear as He speaks as though they were at His side.

There is a calm, a stillness. Yet there is a fragrance and, seemingly, the sound of life coming from every living thing which is present. The sound unites to become at one with the Master's words as He speaks...

BE OPEN AND RECEPTIVE IN SPIRIT
Blessed are the poor in spirit,
for theirs is the kingdom of heaven.

Be open and receptive in spirit:
Then yours is the blessings of the Father in abundance.

What manner of meaning is in these words that the Master has given? For surely it is not that He would ask thee that thou would be in want in any sense. Nor would He, by His nature, expect thee to decline the joys of the Father and the abundance of life in the Earth or any realm.

If thou art in spirit poor, there is the opening for an in-filling of His presence. If there is an intensity of self, if there is that which is called ego, then some might, through the eyes of Earth, see this as wealth or riches. So as, then, that their spirit is filled with illusion, that their desires, their goals, bind them to that which is temporal and of that illusion. Let yourselves (as do we) be open in spirit. Let there not be the presence of any abundance which is false. Let there be an ear to hear spiritually that which is eternally present. As we find it given, here is the

Master's message to you, Brethren, claim for thyself the Light within. Cast off that which would cloud this Light. Cleanse, remove, purify; and let this, the vastness of thy presence within, receive the abundance which is eternal. Spirit is that force which is eternal. Heaven is the description given for that which is achievement and oneness with God. If there be not a vessel, there can be no retention of the spirit.

CONDUCTOR: Give an example of being poor in spirit.

LAMA SING: A man might come to thee and make claims against thee, and these claims may be false. But if you recognize that the entity is struggling within himself, if you recognize that the entity has some image of himself which he must protect and which he must honor above all, then thee can accept his comments without affirming them, for thy spirit is pure, and the image within needs no illusion. It needs no nourishment from Earth, for it is pure from God.

So it is that, if your spirit is poor, it is also receptive. If your spirit is rich in those terms, it can be filled with the illusion of self, as the individual and as the temporal.

CONDUCTOR: The Beatitudes are difficult for me to understand in many, many respects. And I feel they are for many. When it is stated, again, "Blessed are the poor in spirit, for theirs is the kingdom of heaven," it sounds as if, when our spirits are poor, we will inherit the kingdom of heaven.

LAMA SING: We understand. The word poor is extracted from the Greek, which was the translation. It does not mean impoverished. It does not mean destitute; it means, rather, open, receptive.

The literal was, blessed are thou whom art receptive in spirit, for theirs is surely the kingdom of God; and therein shall the blessings of the eternal Spirit of the Father be found in abundance for all who might behold them. That is the literal. So it is the translation to the word poor which causes the difficulty. It should have been and was, Blessed art those who are receptive in spirit, that are open, that are receiving.

BE FORGIVING OF SELF AND OTHERS

**Blessed are they that mourn,
for they shall be comforted.**

Release, forgive self, and know all is intended for growth:
Then the Comforter shall enter and bring understanding.

If thou art capable of understanding light and darkness, if thou have experienced joy and sorrow, if there is the awareness within your consciousness of such things, then there can be the bringing forth of that presence through the Christ which lifts and provides strength.

To mourn is not to weep or lament because of a loss for self. But it is to reconsider and evaluate in comparison to thine own ideal and purposes in life and to weigh these and to review those things which have been perpetuated or done which are not in accord with your own wishes. Then by the action of mourning there is the release of guilt.

If you can forgive yourself, then you can recognize God's presence. If you cannot examine yourself clearly and openly, then there is the tendency to hold self or bind self into the individual sense, and this tends to close or cloud and makes for a lack of ease. But if you can, with joy, release those emotions, those doubts, and those judgments from within self, then the Spirit of God therein will enter.

One who mourns is not one who (by your translation) may necessarily be doing something good or bad; they are simply in mourning. Their reasons or causes for mourning might well be extremely varied. As an example, one who knows that, in past, one of their brethren called out to them for assistance and this one, for reasons which were important at that time, denied this assistance to the entity, may have grievous cause to mourn. But would they mourn for the entity who was in need, or would they be saddened in mourning because they had missed an opportunity to serve in the name of the Christ?

You see, it is not so that an entity should weep and thrash

about, but that the attitude within self should be one which has relegated opportunity, challenge, service, into its proper position within the consciousness. This is, as well, to eliminate frustration, to eliminate anger, to make self, as the newly furrowed field, receptive to those seeds. But if there is the retention of guilt, remorse, or hostility, then nothing can enter in. There cannot be that which is sown.

In your present Earth plane, to mourn is to ask, to release, what you call, limitation. To mourn is to shed self of that which is false, to recognize that all of your experiences, be they good or bad by your judgment, are intended for growth. And then if they must, let your attitude of mourning be a joyful mourning, that thee should truly claim your right to be at one with God.

The Nature of Giving

CONDUCTOR: Lama Sing, you stated in the example that perhaps someone would ask us for help, and at that particular time, or such, that we did not give that. I believe this gives me a better understanding of what you've been trying to explain so many times, that we should wait for them to ask for that help and not volunteer because we feel they need help and thus interfere with their karmic, or, rather, their opportunity-for-growth pattern. Would you clarify that, please?

LAMA SING: This relates to the first Beatitude, as well. For if you are cleansed of spirit, if you are receptive of spirit, then you have an openness and you can hear.

You can ask for the opportunity, and as an entity is observed in want, you can mourn for them. You can beseech the Father to send thee. You can plead lovingly and understandingly for Him to use thee as His vehicle of blessing. Then surely the Comforter shall be with thee and shall, through thee, do those works of His name.

It is well that one understands, life in the Earth plane is for the growth of each soul. There must be the asking before one gives. As thou art asked, then give what thou have, be it a prayer, a loving grasp or embrace, or service to their need; but do so only if it is in accord with thy spirit which is receptive.

CONDUCTOR: In "Blessed are they that mourn, for they shall be comforted" ...how does this comfort come? Is this a sense of peace and tranquility that one has in his life?

The Nature of Comfort

LAMA SING: Yes, and moreover, it is understanding. For as thee are in a state of review of self and as there are found those aspects of self which fall short of your goal, your objective, or that of your ideal, then thee must not hold these against self. And at that point (as you are in this state of review) the Spirit of God brings understanding. It is the Spirit of God, which is the Comforter.

BE IN ASKANCE FOR HIS WILL

**Blessed are the meek,
for they shall inherit the Earth.**

Ask for His Will, and rest in the Presence:
Then yours is the dominion over your experience.

If thee go forward in your life experience commanding this and that, and if thee make demand upon others and self, there is built a wall of great thickness and depth. This wall, then, contains a great strength of purpose and goal. It is not to say that this is bad or good. It is to state that this is intense. So intense can this as a purpose or goal in life become that one's vision spiritually and physically becomes obscured or narrowed. One can tread upon the flowers in the field, in the meadow, or one can pause and touch them and admire them. Both entities will travel to a distant objective. One would be enriched by the experience, the other moves only with a haste born by desire of Earthly accomplishment.

Meekness: this is a translated term, which can be defined in many ways. The Earth is the symbol of achievement, the opportunity, the promise, and the goal. Those who allow their spirit to be at rest, to be meek before the presence of God, to be in askance of His work, then so shall He give to these entities all His joyous works and the domain of the sphere of Earth in which to do them.

It is as He promises, that the Earth is thine for His Children. But those who seek with such a strength of illusion so as to cloud this gentleness, this compassion, and this receptivity will know not, then, to be present, for their goals and desires obscure that of the reality of God's kingdom.

CONDUCTOR: It is very difficult to understand why these were written such as they were and hard to understand. I've gone over them many, many times and perhaps at the time I just wasn't ready to understand. I don't know.

The Greatest Guidance in Written Form

LAMA SING: To understand that they are written as, perhaps, the greatest guidances that remain in your Earth plane in written form. The Beatitudes exist. The Master's discussion from the mount are living thoughts, examples with which to guide each of you unto the kingdom of God.

They are written at several levels: the outer which applies to the physical or material and gives comfort to those whom know only this level of consciousness; and to the inner wherein that of the adept (those of the students whom are receptive and searching for their eternal nature) might find through translation and meditation a clear and concise direction with which to flow in their life. Had they been in different terms, they would have, perhaps, been abolished from the writing by the tribunal. As they presently exist, they have meaning for those whom seek meaning, and they have descriptive guidance for those whom see only this.

This does not mean that there is only one way to interpret these words or these thoughts as they live in spiritual form, for there is an interpretation for each entity whom perceives them.

A child has a delightful enthusiasm, interest, and receptivity because they are meek. They are meek because they have no conscious life experience with which to block or cloud truth and reality when they see it. They have not builded a wall of self-image about self which must be maintained. They are in closer contact or oneness with their spirit, and thus they are meek. You see?

BE IN THIRST FOR YOUR RIGHT PATH WITH GOD
**Blessed are they which do hunger and thirst
after righteousness,
for they shall be filled.**

Hunger for the completion of your right path with God:
Then you shall be filled within and without.

This is, perhaps, one of the clearest guidances given by the Master. For righteousness is, by the comparison of your own ideal, that if you strive, if your very life is to be enhungered or in thirst for the completion of those goals established within your own spirit, then His promise is that ye shall be fulfilled. If thee will seek, thee shall find. If you ask, it shall be given unto thee. This all relates, one and the same, to this statement.

Be Not Idle
It also means: Be thee not idle in your works. Languor not in an attitude of inactivity, for if there be that which could be called sinful, it would, among all gathered here, be concurred that this might, indeed, be the action of inactivity. If there is opportunity, grasp it. As in the Earth plane at present, there is a desire for growth. Each of you seeks now by listening to these words to find some meaning, something with which you might relate within. You are hungered; you are thirsting for what we call righteousness.

The Meaning of Righteousness
What does this word righteousness mean? Does it mean that in a dispute you are correct and the others are in error? That you are upon a proper pathway, as opposed to those which

are erroneous? That you live in an attitude which is perfect, as opposed to that which violates the law of the land? Perhaps in some ways these statements are true. But the righteousness of spirit is of that which the Master speaks, that thy spirit would be set aright, that your mind and your spirit would live in harmony, in service to God.

These are joyful teachings, dear friends, and perhaps our comments are a bit heavy and weighted. The delight of a small child is to know what task lies before them and to seek out with exuberance the completion of it to the satisfaction of those whom dominate their life, be this parent, teacher, counselor, guide. Thou art children, and if you know that which is expected of thee, you can achieve it. So, blessed are those who desire with their very existence to know their purpose, their goal, to know the way. You see?

CONDUCTOR: The thing that is so hard to decide is, what is righteous? What is correct, what is not correct? Many times we are led on many paths that we think are correct, that are righteous at the time, and perhaps find out later that they are not. How does one decide?

The Nature of Righteousness

LAMA SING: By striving, hungering, for righteousness within. Do not base your sense of accomplishment or righteousness upon that which is without, for this is the result; but rather, from within, for here is the cause, the force, which is perfect. You cannot be responsible for the result, but you have the opportunity to commence, at least, with a good intent. So, strive for your proper intent, your proper purpose. If your wish is righteous, then thee shall be rewarded for that which you have done. The attitude and emotion with which you have done this work, this is what is returned to thee.

CONDUCTOR: In other words, if we feel good about it in our heart and we approach it with good feelings and attitudes and emotions, we feel that what we are doing is correct, then there is no ill effect?

LAMA SING: There can never be an ill effect if you truly believe in what you are doing, if your action is based upon humbleness, if it is from pure intent in your spirit. If you are meek or receptive in your way, then what you do is always good. Do not judge the result. Evaluate the effort and intent.

CONDUCTOR: And then they state, for they shall be filled. How is one filled? By inwardly, again, knowing, feeling content, feeling pleased with self? Feeling God is within?

Spiritual Fulfillment

LAMA SING: This and much more. For as you accomplish these various states of spirit, states of mind, states of existence, then you will find that all things will come unto thee as a bearer of His Light. If you are right in your thinking, if you do not have desires which are stronger than your spiritual purpose, if you do not envy or hold hatred or remorse against self, then you shall be fulfilled. How? In every manner that your heart desires.

CONDUCTOR: Lama Sing, again, if I hunger and thirst after righteousness, show me a pathway to righteousness. What should I hunger and thirst after?

A Path of Righteousness

LAMA SING: Where are you at present? Do you know this? Do you know your present state of mind, your present spiritual intent? Have you in this your present Earth day some work which you are about in the Father's name? We shall answer for you: Yes, you do. You are doing this work, at this moment, with the prayerful hope in your spirit that the words which are placed upon this recording device will go forth into the lands of your world and will bear some fruit, some blessing, for those whom perceive them. Then you are pursuing a path of righteousness.

You are, at this moment, deeply hungered spiritually. Your heart thirsts for the accomplishment of this work. Your desire is pure. Your intent is in harmony with the Spirit of the Father, and that is what this means. You will ever, in this lifetime, carry the blessing. You will be ever fulfilled by the accomplishment of this work. For each entity who comes in contact now with that thought which you hold at this moment shall, by their thankfulness, build a thought, an image, which is returned to you without your conscious knowledge. So it is by your work – by your struggle, in effect – to be fulfilled, to satiate your hunger, your thirst, it is by that effort that you are filled. For it is, again, the intent. It is the desire of spiritual service to God that, in and of itself, is the asking. And He has promised He will give to those who ask.

BE KIND TO SELF AND OTHERS
Blessed are the merciful,
for they shall obtain mercy.

Be kind and compassionate to self and others
in thought as well as deed:
Then you shall yourself be graced with God's mercy.

This, perhaps, the easiest of all to comprehend, for if thee can show mercy, then it is thine. It need not be given to thee.

What He is telling thee is that those who use this mechanism of love must first possess it in order to give it. No entity is nourished from an empty cup, only one which is filled with the blessed wine of life. Only these can give.

Where would one commence, then, with showing mercy? Self. Have thee, dear friend, been merciful this day to self? Hast thou chastised self without good cause or reason? Have you burdened your mind, your spirit, with some attitude, with some punishment, with some perceived flaw or fault? Have you, by comparative judgment of self to others or to mass thought or habit, made for yourself an attitude which is less than joyful for this day?

Blessed are the merciful... Be merciful, be understanding, compassionate with self, that by so doing you can give this to others, that you can teach by your manner, by your very presence, that others shall welcome the opportunity for understanding which comes about through experience. If you lack mercy, you also lack joy. For only in compassionate understanding and by forgiveness can one make room for joy. This, among all the rest, must be remembered. Blessed, indeed, are those who show mercy to themselves and thusly to others, for they shall, indeed, be eternally graced with His mercy, as well.

CONDUCTOR: There are yet things in my life that I do not feel that I am merciful about, things that I do not understand, comprehend, or accept and cannot feel a compassionate forgiveness but, rather, a frustration, a bit of anger. How does one overcome things in order to be, then, completely merciful toward all attitudes? Perhaps if this was attained, I would no longer need to be on the Earth plane but had completed all. Is that correct?

Becoming Truly Compassionate

LAMA SING: If you could truly be merciful, would you not have to first have become loving? Would you not have to be humble? Would you not have to be, in effect, poor or receptive in spirit? Would you not have to be forgiving? Would you not have to be humble? You would have some degree and generally a large amount of same of each of these and more. For mercy requires justification.

Your mind functions quite a bit (lovingly, as we see it) in this manner: Well, I have performed this action; and thus now, as I compare this action to what I now know, I believe that was in error. I committed this act, and now I am not pleased with it. Isn't that what you are saying? Can you go back to that action and change it? It would be very difficult in the literal sense of the Earth plane for you to so do, but you spiritually can go back to that action, review it, and understand it.

Understand what emotion, what desires, were involved, and you can, as though you are viewing someone else, express understanding and forgiveness.

If you would look at the past as though you are looking at many different lifetimes, these lifetimes are completed. They have given you an opportunity to grow by understanding the effect and influences of those experiences. You are no longer that entity, for you have slept and you have awakened. You have been reborn, and this day, as you measure it, is a new lifetime, a new opportunity. Through mercy, through the understanding that there is compassion within you, you can release this. It is important for you to do this. It is important for you to forgive these aspects in yourself, for only through this can you truly forgive others.

CONDUCTOR: I will have to go over that carefully to obtain a better understanding of what you're saying to me.

LAMA SING: Let us place these words, then, before thee, for this is among the most important of all. Any action, which you perform, do you comprehend that God understands and still loves thee?

CONDUCTOR: Yes.

LAMA SING: Do you truly believe that He loves thee no matter what you do?

CONDUCTOR: Yes.

LAMA SING: How could He do this? For God is all knowing and all wise. He knows thee as you were, as you are, and He knows what you shall become. If He yet loves thee, then must He not know that ultimately you will become perfect? Can you not, as well, accept that you shall become this perfect being that He sees you as? Then you must know that each experience is a step-stone to the next and the next, and you will repeat those needed as often as you wish.

Time is the illusion of measurement linearly in the Earth plane. Its purpose is for order in your consciousness. Beyond that, time is multi-dimensional and exists in all directions simultaneously. What this means is that you are, at this moment, perfect. You need only to travel your chosen pathway to enable yourself to recognize this perfection. That is what life is generally composed of.

CONDUCTOR: Then if I become more merciful and more forgiving towards self, I can then apply this towards others and other situations that I do not feel I am merciful in?

LAMA SING: Yes, of course, easily so. For what you are saying is, "Well, if they can do this or that, then I can, as well, do similarly" and that is an error. They may do as they wish (they being anyone in your life). Let them as they will, but for thee, follow that which is the guidance within, and you shall always be aright.

It Begins with Self

So if you are merciful to yourself, you have the capacity, then, for mercy to others. You tend to equate in a sense of balance. You weigh this side, then that. If the side which is self is always filled, then your tendency is to attempt to fill the other, the outer, as well.

CONDUCTOR: I believe that I have an understanding of that now, Lama Sing, and I feel truthfully within myself that I feel mercy toward others in different situations. It is, then, when I feel that they should have an understanding of what is correct or incorrect and do not change it, the frustration that I feel with them is their not changing it. And then I have the lack of mercy because I feel that they should know better.

Parable of the Mountain Pathway

You are upon a pathway, which winds about a mountain. It is a very narrow pathway, and it requires that only one or several entities can walk up the pathway abreast. As you, climbing the mountain, turn about and see the others stretched below thee, winding to and fro all the way back down along the mountain and down into a valley... If that valley be, indeed, the valley of darkness, and if you are climbing towards God upon a mountain of experience, looking down at the others who are below thee, you can indeed state to them, "Oh, thee below, why did thee not start thy journey earlier, that you might be here with me at this moment?" To which their response would be meaningless because you cannot comprehend from their level because you have gone beyond it. You do not see the clouds that surround them, that they must move slowly to find the pathway carefully and not fall from it, for you are moving moreso into the light.

But now you turn again and cast your gaze to the pathway, and someone from far above you speaks down forcefully, "Oh, thee, entity beneath me, why hast thou not commenced thy effort sooner, that thou might now be here with me at this level from whence I can see much better than thee and where it is warmer and more beautiful?" How, then, shall thee answer?

CONDUCTOR: I believe I understand, and I thank those for having understanding and mercy for me.

Receiving Compassion from Others

And that is the meaning of this teaching. Being merciful is having the ability to envision yourself at lesser levels upon the mountain of experience, and by having compassion for those who are struggling as have thee. By expressing this mercy, this compassion, those above will reach their hands down to thee and help thee, for thee are growing and moving faster than you can physically climb. Thus they will assist. Your gift that you give determines the gift that you receive.

BE THE CHANNEL FOR GOD'S BLESSISNGS
Blessed are the pure in heart,
for they shall see God.

Ask for and bring forth God's blessings in all your actions:
Then you shall perceive Godliness in all.

The heart is the center of one's desire and consciousness. If, within your desire, there is purity – purity defined as the understanding of your ideal and the willingness to pursue it – if your heart is pure, this means that you are in askance of His blessings and His work.

Parable of the Marketplace

It is as one in a marketplace who attempts to find a value for his goods. Before he opens his booth, he walks to and fro in the marketplace, and he examines similar goods from other merchants. One merchant asks what you determine to be a very excessive amount for his goods.

You ask him straight away, "Oh, kind sir, I admire thy goods; but for what reason are they so dear in price?"

The merchant responds humbly, "See, dear friend, I am withered in this, my left arm, and as I labor in the weaving of this garment, I require three days time to complete one garment. Am I not then to be paid for my effort, or is it that I shall be paid for the result? The goodness of this cloth, the fabric, all of these things speak for my tradesmanship."

Satisfied with this comment, you travel further, and you come to another booth. And here yet another merchant with similar goods asks a completely different price, far less than the other. You speak to him, "Kind sir, for what reason does thou ask this lowly price for your goods? As I examine them, they appear to be of goodness, of moderate texture."

He responds, "Kind sir, God has blessed me with abundance. I have many children, a very kind and supportive mate. It is not my hands alone that labor to produce these goods, but united, we, a family, produce them in great abundance. Many of these each day are completed by our joyous labors together. Would it not be well, then, that I should share and make these available to all who have need of their warmth?"

Satisfied with this answer, you return to your own booth. As you select your garments from their container and place them for display, then, how shall thee determine what price you shall ask for yours? Blessed, indeed, are the pure at heart.

Ask, then, of each who wishes one, whatsoever they can give, for their need alone is sufficient for thy labor. Then thee shall see God.

Purity of heart is the desire to fulfill and bring joy to others. If your heart is open, loving, and serves where it is needed, gives to those who are in want, and accepts from those who desire to give, then you are just, you are humble, you are pure of heart, you are capable of mourning, you are indeed thirsting for righteousness. You see? Each teaching builds upon itself and leads to the next and to the next.

CONDUCTOR: Since I am not in dressmaking or cloth making of any kind, as of your example, Lama Sing, how can I be more pure at heart?

LAMA SING: The merchant that we described offered to others that which he had. Ask yourself often, "What have I to give?" You have to give whatever another asks of thee. Give to them as you can, and ask of them in return only that which they can give. If thee prepare a cake and you know of one who has desire for same, then by the pureness of your heart give to them. If thee have tamed a bird of song and you know that there is one who has a heart which is saddened, then give that song, a gift to them if they ask, and know that their heart shall ever be filled.

But you know within yourselves, each of you, what you have to give, and you know very well those who are in need. Give love, give compassion, give forgiveness, and more.

CONDUCTOR: There is something that I would like to have clarification of in this regard... giving. At times I feel that sometimes in giving it is sometimes more harmful to the individual than it is good. How does one decide this?

Knowing How and When to Give

By the spirit within. For God will guide thee to know when it is aright and when it is a perpetuation of error on the part of the receiver. For some will ask of thee again and again, without effort and without desire, only that they would perpetuate their lot with no desire for growth or for enrichment of experience. Then to these, give in accordance with the knowledge within, for there shall not be the wasting of the pearls before swine. You must not judge self but, rather, ask of your own spirit. Then have the faith to claim that your spirit is true because you are at one with God. And as it is asked of spirit within thee to give, then thou must.

CONDUCTOR: How can one truly feel pure at heart, when it is many times these same people that need more help than the others? And yet you have to deny that giving because it is not helping though they really need it.

Knowing What to Give

You must give the gift that is appropriate for the need. If the need appears, then answer it, but answer it with the greatest gift that thou possess: give them opportunity or prayer or blessing, that they might find light and that they might find joy. But also be humble, be meek. Know that their lot is chosen by them. Remember, thou art upon a mountain of experience. Your position on the pathway is different than theirs. If an entity far below asks thee, "Pass me a vine, a rope, that I might ascend directly without following this path turning to and fro so endlessly to reach thy present position," shall thee pass the rope down to the entity?

CONDUCTOR: If they sincerely seek, yes, I would.

LAMA SING: Then if they reach your point, they will have missed the experiences that you have had, the experiences that have given thee the strength to continue on. They will be wearied. They will require rest. And you will leave them behind once again. As you must continue, only to turn about one moment and see them once again far below thee pleading to thee, "Throw me but a rope that I might ascend to thy present position and be with thee." You see? Cast them not a rope but give them a strong light, that they might see in the darkness of their present level. Give them a light which illuminates their footsteps, that they can tread moreso and moreso swiftly. Give them a prayer, within which creates a buoyancy which will lift them rapidly up that pathway. Give them a rope, yes, but let it be forged of the fibers of spirit.

So if an entity asks of thee, indeed do respond. Give them

what you can, but give to them something of light, something of purpose, for them within. Prayer is the greatest blessing one entity can give to another, save for love itself.

Seeing, Knowing, Experiencing God

CONDUCTOR: As stated, Blessed are the pure in heart, for they shall see God, what does this mean... we will see God? Visually? Or we will know Him? Feel His presence within us?

LAMA SING: Yes. It means, by your actions, by your works, by your intent, you shall reach a point of awareness wherein you realize what God is... wherein you begin to actually experience oneness with God. You see? It is not so much so that one would literally see an image fashioned in the manner of man and know that image to be God, for that has not the importance in this statement. It is that you shall see the state of Godliness, that you shall perceive and be at one with the existence of God, that you shall command those forces which are in accord with God, that you might do all manner of work as the Master's pure heart enables Him to do and as He still does.

Blessed are the pure of heart: Blessed is the intent, for this shall accomplish the goal, the ideal. Blessed are the pure of heart: Blessed are those whose inner being is a light to others. Blessed are the pure in heart, for they shall see God: for they shall see themselves. Blessed are those who are willing to seek and to accept, for they shall know. All of these apply.

BE HARMONIOUS WITH ALL

**Blessed are the peacemakers,
for they shall be called the children of God.**

Be harmonious with all, knowing God in all:
Then you will truly know and employ your heritage
as a Child of God.

In this, one might find an interpretation which tends to isolate or narrow the beautiful effect of this guidance from the

Master. To be a peacemaker is also to be one who has not that emotive self which reacts to stimuli or emotion in a manner which is as to protect self, or to protect the image of self as it has been projected. Thus one can make peace or create an environ which is in harmony by avoiding reaction to stimuli which might under other circumstances promote disharmony, aggression, hostility, anger, even those actions of aggression or war between men and peoples.

To be called a Child of God is to be recognized for your receptiveness, your openness, to be recognized as in accord with the ideal or principles which that entity sees as Godly, and that the observer or that entity sees these in thee sufficient so as to call thee a Child of God. They are speaking to thee, that you uphold in their mind their highest ideal.

So combining this, then (which is actually two clear definitions), a peacemaker is one who receives all experiences in life in an attitude of understanding, of harmony, and of joy. And by that action and attitude they invoke admiration and imitation on the part of others.

Blessed are the peacemakers... Blessed are those who strive for harmony and love between others. Blessed are those who hunger for peace within themselves and, thus, strive to make this condition exist as a part of their life. Then that aspect of themselves which sees God from a unique individual perspective will be able to merge with the aspect of self which is the id or the ego or the identity as it is lived in daily activity. So the inner meaning is clear. Striving for peace, harmony, in your own emotions, in your own activities, enables thee to claim your own inner heritage and recognize yourself as on a proper pathway and in accord with your highest ideal.

You understand, of course, dear friends, what it means to be a child, and you know within yourselves that you are all Children of God. So what can this mean, to be recognized as a Child of God, to be titled as a Child of God? It is clearly that you, yourself, would claim your heritage. If you strive for peace within yourself, you enable the claiming of your own heritage.

CONDUCTOR: Lama Sing, how can we, as just ordinary individuals in everyday life, be peacemakers?

Being an Everyday Peacemaker

LAMA SING: A very good question, for it's an important aspect of your present environ in the Earth plane. There are, of course, many experiences in the Earth plane which could promote the condition you call anger. Often you are angered at another entity's actions because they are not in conformance with what you consider to be, for example, good manners, good etiquette, good spiritual purpose or intent. They may, in their actions, violate some of the laws of your lands. Or they may, indeed, violate the teachings of the Master and (as it is given) the Word of God. How, then, can one avoid reacting in a hostile, angry way?

To be sure, we understand this can be difficult. But if you begin at this point, we believe (humbly) you will find it becomes easier and easier to be a peacemaker.

Seeing the Total Creation

There is an aspect within yourself that judges, evaluates, and then reacts on the basis of that judgment. We have stated to you many times in past, "Judge only by your own ideal, your own series of goals, your own purposes for life; do not base your judgments upon the actions or the requirements of others, for each is uniquely beautiful and individual." Based upon that, then, you must understand that some entities act in accordance with their own frustration. They act in accordance with a lack of faith. They may react out of emotion or fear. But that is not the entity; that is, rather, the reaction to existing conditions.

If you see the entity as a total creation of God, you cannot avoid seeing also that entity's potential. Now you can respond to an affronting situation in a manner which is calm, tranquil, and requires not the taking of positions or sides. This can be done by simply observing, for a moment, a period of silence, asking God to guide your words, your actions, and your deeds.

Avoid Reaction

Remembering the climb upon the mountain of experience and, from where that entity might be located, their view of life (which is the valley below you) is different. Thus they deal with life in a manner which they know, based upon their experiences and their attitudes at that point. So then, do not react from their level, as they have acted from a level of consciousness. React only from your own level of consciousness, not theirs. If they are harsh, show them what love is. If they are angry, show them what joy is. It cannot withstand your faith, your confidence in God.

In short then, by avoiding reaction because you are calm, because you have claimed your heritage, then you eliminate the potential for a condition other than a joyous, peaceful one. This does not mean that you should avoid what we would call your position in life. You have the right of claiming your own pathway. You have no need to defend it, and you have no need to justify its existence. It is, because it is what you have chosen. See?

CONDUCTOR: Very well, Lama Sing. As it was stated, Blessed are the peacemakers, for they shall be called the Children of God, and as you have stated, we are all Children of God. Knowing this, then, it would not be important to be called a Child of God. It wouldn't be any special acclamation or anything, because it is special already, because we already are. Would you help me with a better understanding?

Being an Example of the Light

LAMA SING: What you have stated is, of course, true. But you see, it is, to the entity who is observing, important for them to recognize this quality in others, for it helps them to recognize its potential and its presence within themselves. And so that is important, that you are recognized, in that sense, by others, for that is showing them the Light of His presence within thee.

Perhaps an appropriate example here might be what you call a feud. Two families, for some obscure infraction of one another's rights, as they were believed, long in the past, have created an attitude of a feudal condition between the family groupings. Generation to generation continues to despise or hate or even resort to violence against the other family. The actual cause may be long lost in obscurity of the passage of your Earth time. Yet within them, there is an emotion, which is directed towards the other grouping.

As Within, So Without

A peacemaker is one who does not tolerate such a condition to exist within themselves. That two factions of self might be considered as two families feuding over some obscure event in the past. This might be called the factions of right and wrong. This might be the factions of self and those forces apart from self. This might simply be a desire within self, which is unfulfilled.

By allowing that both aspects within you can exist and have their rightful purpose, you take away the cause of the hostility of one to the other.

Now this has profound meaning in the outer, as well. For if a faction within self struggles against another faction, then in each experience that you encounter, you will tend to evaluate your choices from two different positions. It is important that you be unified within in order to perceive each opportunity from its total sense.

Meet Each Opportunity with Joy

Many entities have a very disruptive life pattern because they are viewing each situation in such a manner. They are torn, listless, emotive. They are having difficulty justifying any decision that they make regarding an opportunity. To meet an opportunity with a joyous service or work is to be a Child of God. In order to accomplish this, you must make peace within yourself. Then you are a Child of God.

Understand that, in a manner of speaking, God does not essentially need your help. But He wants to give you His help. He has need of your request. He has need of your desire, because He wills that your consciousness is precious, inviolate. God desires to help you and has the need for you to ask... need in the sense of a loving patience, a loving desire, a loving joy, not in the sense of an emotive need based on the Earth plane's understanding.

Understand One Another and Make Peace

If you see an entity in anguish, frustration, be a peacemaker and show them the way. Ask God to guide, as they have asked of thee for assistance. If they have not asked thee, then be an example. Do not tell them do this or that, but show them by the example.

You have conflicts in the Earth plane. These conflicts are because of different positions on the mountain, as we have described it. Each of you sees your lives from a different position. But if you can reach beyond your position to understand one another, then you are making peace: first, within self because you are willing; then, within others because you are doing.

CONDUCTOR: Lama Sing, does God have no needs of any kind? Is everything complete with and for Him, and He simply gives all He has for everyone else, for His Children?

Helping God

LAMA SING: We speak as the servants of God through the name of the Christ. We do not wish that there would be the thought that these words are God's, but from the consciousness of God we perceive the answer. Humbly...

God, indeed, has no needs in the sense of your perspective in the Earth plane. He has needs from the aspect that He wishes each of you to claim your heritage. He desires that each of you would recognize your own divine and infinite existence. To say that He longs for this would be inappropriate, for there is no measure of time as we see it, and thus, one cannot equate a sense of longing as you would equate it by measure of time. See? But, rather, that He wishes at this moment that each of thee could know Him, by way of knowing yourselves and knowing that He is present within you.

You help God by helping yourselves and others.

Here is an example, perhaps, which will more clearly answer your question: If thee as a parent see one of your children in an experience in their life struggling desperately to meet that challenge and to accomplish it, you know that from your position of wisdom and experience and accomplishment in your own life that you could easily step in, intercede for your child, and accomplish the task they are trying to perform. Isn't that so, often?

And if you do that again and again and again, what will happen? They will not learn. They will not master their own abilities. And isn't that even so when they are crying out in anguish or emotion when their heart has been broken at the loss of something which is loved? Or the failure to achieve something which is desired?

Companions and Co-Creators with God

This and more could be given, but there is no need. It is that God perceives thee as His children and as His companions. When you are willing to claim your heritage, you will be beyond children. you will be co-creators with God.

When you have accomplished this, then we shall all join together and create realms of infinite beauty and love. There shall be existence and joy such as your minds cannot conceive. Your very life shall be filled with music, with warmth, with radiance, with love. You shall have about you whatever your heart conceives as beautiful. You shall communicate with all things, and know them, and they shall know thee. There would be harmony between that which exists in your realm and all other realms. Those things which are hostile in your present environ would be loving, kind. There would be compatibility among all things. There would be no sorrow, no weariness, no dis-ease, nothing which would be less than perfect. God wants this for each of thee, when thou art ready.

CONDUCTOR: Lama Sing, does God ever become discouraged with us? Like you were saying, that we are the parents of children and we can help them, and God is like our Father and we are His Children and He can help us. Does He ever become discouraged with us? Does, perhaps, He intercede with some of the things that are taking place on the Earth plane at this time so that we can learn and grow, such as Iran and such. Or are these created by our own hand? Do you understand what I am trying to say?

God Never Wearies of Us

LAMA SING: We see your thoughts, yes. God knows all of these things, of course, and is, by His omnipotent presence, a part of all of these things, simply a use of energy towards your desires, your goals, and your mass-thought.

He has those who have claimed their heritage, who function in accord with His Will. There are those at varying levels of acceptance who are continuing to work and to raise their consciousness, that they might be at one with God. Many of these gain in experience and consciousness by helping you in the Earth plane and others, and it is in these realms that the concern is often found.

God does intercede in accordance with His Will, His plan. He takes action to create conditions which are best for all His Children. Just as you provide shelter, food, clothing, and experience for your children, God provides thee, each of thee, these selfsame things. Does He weary of this? Never. We might state it is His desire, and thus it could be, in a manner of speaking, His longing, that each of thee would claim your heritage now, that there would not be the need of further experience of such a nature as causes any sadness to any soul. But that growth would be by understanding and not by experience of sadness.

CONDUCTOR: Lama Sing, how can we people become

peacemakers in places like, precisely at this time, Iran and Afghanistan? What can we do?

The Nature of Peace Consciousness

LAMA SING: If thee would gather twenty pure of heart and if these twenty would pray in the Master's name with sincerity and in proper accord, this matter would dissolve. See?

Regarding the topic of making peace, it is first to understand what the nature of peace is in the minds, hearts, in the consciousness of others. Without the knowledge of what their concept of peace or happiness or tranquility is, one might have a very difficult time in so perpetuating this, even as an opportunity for them. So one must be knowledgeable of those they seek to serve. There must be an open receptiveness to their emotions, their thoughts, their attitudes, in order to function clearly in a manner which promotes their concept of peace.

The absence of hostility or aggression is not necessarily a state of peace. One can be completely devoid of fears of physical harm, physical aggression, emotional punishment, or any sort of aggression in any manner whatever, and still not be at peace within themselves. So, helping another entity to gain a state of peace is helping them to gain grace, helping them to claim their rightful heritage as Children of God, growing, becoming at one with the Father. And this is best done, as always, by perpetuating the living example of that which you know to be truth and that which you know to be a situation which promotes, creates peace.

In such a manner, then, you would be recognized for your light and your wisdom, and it would be known that this would be coming forth from God. And there would be thanks unto God; and you yourselves would claim your rightful heritage as His Children, in addition to their recognition at various levels of this fact. By perpetuating that state of peace first within yourselves and then, by the example, in others, you can eliminate those energies which are now at work in the Earth and which can have disruptive effect to the Earth itself, as well as to those environs and entities thereupon.

BE TRUE TO THE PATH
**Blessed are they that are persecuted
for righteousness' sake,
for theirs is the kingdom of heaven.**
As you are tested by others, stay true to the path:
Then you are a co-creator with God.

Approaching this statement by the Master from its reverse, heaven is that state of being wherein all forces are in harmony, and kingdom is that which you as an individual have control over. Thus, combining this, it promotes for the state of control over your own domain, your own happiness, your own existence in harmony.

Now then, blessed are they that art persecuted... Entities will attempt to disrupt thee often from thy work, from thy ideal. To some extent this is an occurrence caused by forces which are in harmony with thee, in order to strengthen thee even moreso to be in accord with that which you believe, that which is righteous. Other entities will persecute those who cling to their own oneness with God, their righteousness, because they wish to test it. Because, within themselves, they too desire to have such a faith, such a dedication; and often they feel, they believe, that by challenging this, they will prove it to be either real and factual or simply an illusion. Their inner desire is that they can prove it to be correct and that they, too, can become a part of its existence.

About the Father's Work
So you are actually, by being persecuted, doing one of the Father's greater works. It gives one the example to place into reality all of the teachings which have been given above and all of those aspects of same which are known to thee from the other comments and guidances from the Master. So you are, indeed, blessed when you are persecuted for the Light.

Righteousness is right thinking, a right path, a correct manner of harmony, a correct experience which is perpetuated by the influences and tendencies collectively assembled by all of your life experiences. So it is an opportunity to strengthen, and it is, indeed, a blessing for you.

Blessed are they who are persecuted... Blessed are they who are challenged. Blessed are Children of Light when they are placed in those environs which afford them the opportunity to do their work. They, then, shall be co-creators with God.

This might be another manner of speaking those same thoughts... If an entity in the physical sense is persecuted of the physical body, their mind and their spirit yet remain free. If an entity is persecuted of the mind, their spirit even yet remains free. The spirit can only submit of its own accord.

Righteousness Is the Infinite Power

Thus, righteousness is so important. It is the infinite power. It is the very spirit of self. If you voluntarily give up your righteousness, then this can, indeed, change your entire physical, mental, and spiritual existence, where you have no longer a reference point. But if you claim your righteousness, if you claim your image, then no matter what encounter you shall have, this will always be your light, and then you command or you have the kingdom of heaven, which is the power. See?

CONDUCTOR: How can we do this in a better way? How can we hold to this? Can you give us some examples?

LAMA SING: Holding to this often requires the use, methodically and continually, of all of the guidance given previously. It is the accomplishment of one's state of being. As you are in a state of existence which is to receive scorn or to be physically, mentally, emotionally suppressed by another, you can endure this if your spirit, your strength, is high.

If you are in accord with right thinking, if you are in harmony with the Master's Light, often others will persecute you because they have not been able to accept this way of living themselves. If you express love to them, if you express the ideal, the light, the completeness of what you believe, you shall, throughout eternity, bear the light of that work. One must often raise their perspective beyond the Earth plane in order to truly place this teaching into activity. See?

As Christ's Own

Blessed are ye when men shall revile you and persecute you and shall say all manner of evil against you falsely for my sake…When you have claimed the Master's work as your own, and when you ask to be sent, to be used in His work, you will meet with those Forces which are, at the least, reluctant to change. And as you go forth doing His work in those realms wherein He has sent you, know that no work is ever done without benefit to you and to those you are serving. Thus you are strengthened, and you grow.

But, you are blessed because you are affronting those Forces which most resist His Light and which need most and which cry out most desperately for guidance, for light. Thus your work and your service in His name is of the purest and brightest of all. And if they commit evil and if they cast untrue things at thee, know that you have met them at a level of their consciousness wherein they can be receptive, for surely they will ignore thee if thou art not approaching a sensitized level of their consciousness. Often one cries out with the greatest of all vigor when approached at a level of their most intense desire.

It is, perhaps, the culmination of the promises that are elucidated in the others. It is, without question, the Master's own promise to you: that no matter where thou art, He is with thee; no matter what work you are about, His strength is thine if you will claim it. Never doubt that He has this love for thee and never feel that thou art alone.

Meeting the Force That Denies Within Self

When you attempt to apply all of those things which we have discussed above, you must ultimately meet within yourself a force which seeks to deny, disprove, discredit, and to disillusion your own consciousness. There will be factions within you that will argue, debate, and have very strong and very firm positions to present to your consciousness, which will attempt to dissuade you from righteousness and from following the workings of the Christ; these will be habit, these will be fear, these will be illusion and other aspects.

But if you continually, in your meditation and in your prayers, ask for strength, ask for Light which is at one with God, that the way is clear and that thou art strong, then even if these struggles take place, they are beautiful, and thee will be called by the Christ as His own. For if you can first wrestle with all of the aggressors within, then what work, ever, can any aggressive force without ever do upon thee? If you can meet each challenge, if you can accept each opportunity presented by the forces within self, then you can meet any faction, any experience, in any realm.

To be called by the Christ as His own, to be recognized, and for Him to prepare a place for thee in the kingdom of God, this means that thou art recognized as having accepted your oneness with God, and karma becomes an experience of past nature to you. It no longer is a needed tool. You will possess grace. You will be able to use grace to serve, even further, others and yourself.

CONDUCTOR: We thank you very, very much, Lama Sing, for giving us a better understanding of the Beatitudes from your viewpoint. I find it very, very helpful to me, and I'm sure others will for themselves also. Is there anything more you would like to state in closing?

CLOSING COMMENTS

LAMA SING: We would ask each of thee to please accept this joyous meeting, not only with the sounds of the words which are spoken through this Channel but also with your hearts open to receive the intent of our joyous works this day, in this meadow with the Master.

It is our eternal prayer that you shall find the joy and happiness of your complete being, that when you are met with challenge, when you must use the meekness of your heart, when your spirit must be as poor, when all of these statements as they are written in the Holy Book are reviewed, let them be spiritually felt within, that the spirit of the Word as given directly from the Master have its import to you.

NOT THE WORDS AS MUCH AS THE SPIRIT IN THEM

Do not dwell upon the verbiage, but claim the spirit, the intent, which lives on throughout eternity and requires no interpretation.

The Beatitudes, the Sermon on the Mount... So many of you were present, so many of you literally experienced what the Master taught. Remember that He is still teaching, right at this moment, right where you are. Will you not pause in the meadow of life to hear His words of love?

We have been filled with honor and joy to have been with thee once again, dear friends; and it is unto the Father and unto the Christ that we give joyous thanks that we might have been called upon to serve in this most humble manner. It is eternally our prayer that these words will live and grow as the flowers of field, as things of beauty and pleasure for you all. Thus we are prepared to conclude, if we are permitted.

CONDUCTOR: I would like to ask one more thing. When we asked you for topics that you would like to speak on to present to the people, you said we should do the Beatitudes. Why did you want to do this, in particular?

LAMA SING: It is very important that each entity in the Earth considers themselves in the nature or manner that the Master has: that they look to themselves as already perfect, and consider life a means by which they can express this perfection, and nothing more. It is not a punishment. It is not that you are guilty of some past sin. It is not that you have been denied by the Christ as one of His own. It is a glorious honor, a blessing, a privilege, to be in the Earth; and it is a wondrous opportunity to become aware of what you already are.

The Earth plane is at a point of some significance in consciousness. Already there has been a very significant improvement (by your method of evaluation, we use that term), so much moreso in some realms, some locales, or areas of your Earth plane are the Forces balanced, that we joyously believe that there will be a significant diminishment of those conflicts which might otherwise have pervaded those areas.

We pray that by some collective knowledge of the immense control that you have over your domain (humbly thought to have been helped by this discussion on the Master's teachings from the mount), it was thusly our prayer and is our belief that this will, in some way, contribute to the furthering of understanding and the balancing of those energies of which we speak. It is entirely possible that only a moderate effect to the western coastal area of North America might now be anticipated. It is possible that even this would occur with such less intensity, that an actual change in the geographic appearance may be either forestalled or eliminated completely.

But nonetheless, the importance here has been to use this period in your consciousness and to use the cycle of movement of your soul grouping (that is, the souls who function in the Earth plane) to reach beyond and to claim your movement along the mountain of experience, that you can move to another realm, to a higher level of your own acceptance. And thus it is our prayer that the cycle will not need be repeated.

CONDUCTOR: We thank you so much, Lama Sing, for your time, your love and your consideration. We surely do appreciate it.

LAMA SING: These things we give from an infinite Source and do so joyously. It is we who thank thee, each one, for this blessed opportunity to have been with you in humble service. Know in your hearts, each one, the strength, the power, of your prayer.

In this, be strong. In this, cling to your heritage.

9 - The Lord's Prayer

CHANNEL/AL MINER: The topic of this reading is the Lord's Prayer, and we would like to thank the individual and the group around her who have submitted this request on behalf of their own studies and as a dedicated work to all who are seeking. I'm requested to read Matthew 6: 9-13, and Luke 11: 1-4. Jesus is speaking, and it is written that He said:

Matthew, Chapter 6:

After this manner therefore pray ye: Our Father which art in heaven, Hallowed be thy name.

Thy kingdom come. Thy Will be done in Earth, as it is in heaven.

Give us this day our daily bread.

And forgive us our debts, as we forgive our debtors.

And lead us not into temptation, but deliver us from evil: For thine is the kingdom, and the power, and the glory, forever. Amen.

And from Luke, Chapter 11:

And it came to pass, that, as He was praying in a certain place, when he ceased, one of his disciples said unto him, Lord, teach us to pray, as John also taught his disciples.

And He said unto them, When ye pray, say, Our Father which art in heaven, Hallowed be thy name. Thy kingdom come. Thy Will be done, as in heaven, so in Earth.

Give us day by day our daily bread.

And forgive us our sins; for we also forgive every one that is indebted to us. And lead us not into temptation; but deliver us from evil.

SPONSOR'S QUESTIONS

Please point out the lessons involved in this prayer and how we may apply these in our daily lives:

1. Did Jesus include a prayer for the dead, as we have read? Can you give the prayer to us as Jesus gave it to His Disciples? Please comment on the circumstances in which the prayer was first given.

2. Is it a good idea to pray the Lord's Prayer focusing on the chakras as it is taught, for example, by the A.R.E., that's the Association for Research and Enlightenment in Virginia Beach? Please comment on this meditation exercise.

3. The Lord's Prayer is, perhaps, the most repeated prayer in the Western world and, I am sure, is often used as "lip service" only. Does the prayer in that case still have a beneficial effect?

4. What effect did the Master intend to produce when He gave the prayer and said, "After this manner therefore pray ye"?

5. Certainly the Lord's Prayer when spoken sincerely produces effects on many levels. Could you discuss these from your perspective so that we may learn to say the prayer with a greater understanding. Please give us anything else you may find to be of benefit to us or points we may have missed for guiding this topic. We thank you for your help, guidance, and prayers, Lama Sing.

LAMA SING COMMENTARY

In considering this prayer, consider the environment, the circumstance, in which it was, for the most part, given. There had been many great works performed, and the multitudes, the peoples, had been gathering for quite some time. Now, as could be seen, their number stretched well beyond one's perception, one's ability to comprehend. As all who were gathered around the Master did see as well, of course, did the Master observe and know that this was that time appropriate to give unto the workers that they might go forth among the multitude and, as is so oft thought, to tend and feed the flock.

So then, not only unto the workers but unto all, this prayer – as ye know it, the Lord's Prayer – was given in its greatest import. Not only this, but much in terms of what can be called the Universal Truth, the universal secret. Indeed, in the wisdom of the Master there was given those tools, which could, by their proper use, set not only the worker, but all, free. These are those tools which liveth on in your time, in your day, in the Earth plane, and shall endure throughout all eternity in one form of expression or understanding or another.

As we seek to provide information in response to your questions, it is not our intent to deter from that as it is written and is so familiar in the hearts and minds of so many of you. It is rather to provide this information as a form of support, encouragement, and perhaps a different perspective of understanding that will enable you to use these gifts even more wisely and more widely.

THE PRAYER IN ITS ESSENCE

Thus, as the Master clearly stated, "After this manner therefore pray ye," it is to be understood from this – then, as now – that a prayer should not be rigid in its recitation or application; that a prayer, as it might be given here or elsewhere, is to be thought of in its essence as a spiritual form, a thought-form, which when one enters in to the ideal, the spiritual concept of it, one becomes a living part of that which they are then expressing.

Be cautioned, as you well know, against the mere recital in a rote, in a dogma, in a redundancy, of such a prayer, so as to ultimately obscure the real meaning of what it is you are attempting to affirm, and to become only as one who performs in accordance to another's will, as commanded by the tug of a cord or string, likened unto a puppet. Be not, then, in idleness when reciting this or any other prayer. If your recitation is verbatim, then think and feel what you are expressing.

We would see the Master's comments – and, indeed, His cautions, which preceded these –to indicate to you and to all the need to adopt this as a form, to adopt this as the spirit of prayer; and to recognize, as He stated, that the Father knoweth that which thou needeth even before thee.

Affirming Aspects of the Prayer in Self

So if you realize that God knows your need before you can even recognize it, and if you know that the Father wishes you to have the greatest of abundance and joy, then it might well follow that the prayer has another very significant purpose other than that which is so widely accepted and left to be its function, its intent. And that is to affirm in self certain aspects, certain tenets, certain qualities, which when they do become a living affirmation enable you to be the channel of the Father's blessings for self and for all of existence.

UNDERSTANDING ITS ELEMENTS

Creator of All

Our Father

Consider that. This is the statement that affirms that unto whom you speak and to whom you pray is the Creator of all and unto which all power is affirmed.

Which is also the best in me

Whom art in heaven

Heaven, then, being thought of perhaps, in one sense, as being the ultimate, as being the purest and highest state of existence, also being thought of as the purest and best as thou art capable of forming in your thought. You are saying, all that is powerful in the highest that I can construe, that I can conceive, the greatest and best within me, for surely if The Father liveth, He liveth within thee. So then is this not, as well, God within me, God in my highest place, that which is best within me? So you are summoning the highest from within. So if you live in an attitude that affirms that God is within and that this is the highest and best, then you will begin to transform your life. You will begin to emanate this aspect, this quality of existence, that it shall first precede you and penetrate all that is your experience, perhaps the most powerful and most blessed affirmation that might be used in any prayer.

I confirm the Power present by affirming Your existence
Hallowed be Thy Name

To state Hallowed be Thy Name is to confirm that the power of God is present merely in the affirmation of His existence, for the name is the calling vibration of any entity, any soul, thing, or that which is in existence. So we are stating here, powerful is Thy presence, Father within, the Highest.

And I pledge myself to You, the one Creative Force

Hallowed be thy name is also an affirmation of loyalty. You are pledging self and self's activities, thoughts, prayers, and intents unto the best, unto that which you consider to be, at least symbolically, the one power, the total Creative Force.

Bring the best and greatest within me into daily life.
Thy kingdom, come. Thy Will, be done.

We are stating here (as can be perhaps concluded from the manner in which we are speaking) that the presence of God becomes that which is our very world. We are asking the best and greatest within ourselves to come into the Earth.

We follow that with an affirmation that this is within. For

heaven is that as one can conceive as the highest ideal, the very best of all in terms of existence and application of Universal Law. We are affirming, then, that we wish to bring our spiritual height into the daily life. We are binding, in essence, spirit, mind, body, emotion, and howsoe'er else ye shall define an aspect of self into a state of oneness, that they shall function as an integral, complete oneness, not as a separateness (referring casually from one to the other) but as a complete expression. We are affirming that we exist in these levels. We are affirming that our expression lives in every essence that exists.

Those who use this prayer and focus upon the levels of power, the levels of creative energy called the chakras, are wise in so doing, in the sense that, properly taken, this can purify each of these levels; cause them to be unified in harmony and balance; and can cause a sensation, an awareness of an energy flowing in great cyclic orbs, uplifting and clearing the mind, preparing self to perceive (or receive, if you prefer) the highest and best guidance as can be given for any need, any purpose unto which you have summoned this state of consciousness.

So we would affirm the wisdom in this, though we would caution here to not so do idly, but to have a purpose for so doing. For one does not summon an entity in the Earth whose abilities are in much demand to answer a call which has no merit for their knowledge, their talent. Likewise, summon not that power – or, if ye prefer, the Father – when there is not that need. For as ye call Him, there are those of service in His name who will respond; and finding no work, they shall be, in that essence, denied a joy, an opportunity. This is not to be overemphasized. It is merely to recognize that, as one performs this, it is good to have a purpose.

We should quickly add here that a very valid purpose is the desire simply to be at one with God and to unify self singularly or in a group effort for a greater good or purpose that the group may have chosen as its work. But have some purpose, some intent... this we should think is good for all, and wise.

Give unto us our every need, our due, the fruit of our labor.

Give us this day our daily bread

Give to us our every need. Father. It is Thee who provideth all that I have and who creates the opportunity for every moment. We are stating in this, again, an affirmation. In essence, this prayer could be thought of as a series of the most powerful affirmations. For the bread is the symbol of the fruit of the earth. It is the symbol of the potential, of the spirit of God found in nature which, when tended and properly nourished, can bear forth fruit or its seed, which, upon its harvest, can sustain the keeper. It is the reflection upon the Universal Law indicating that thee will, thee must, harvest after the seed which thou hast sown.

So we are affirming here, Father, give unto us as is our due. Give unto us now that which is our need. Give unto us this day our daily bread, for it is not the literal bread but, rather, the fruit of thy labor, the harvest of the seeds which thou hast sown. This should have particular emphasis when there is a time (which you would call) of darkness, of need, of sorrow, where the understanding has not provided the light, and the situation is one which is justifiably in need of healing, in need of grace.

See those debts that we do not and forgive us these,

just as we attempt to do as well for others.

Forgive us our debts, as we forgive our debtors

Here, we are affirming that we will cleanse, in this affirmation, all thoughts which deter self from the presence and oneness of God. Remember that we have, at the onset, affirmed God, His existence, His eternal nature; we have affirmed His presence within us, and so forth; and now we are stating that we are cleansing aspects of our being (chakras, if you wish);

but above all else, we are recognizing and applying Universal Law. We are, thusly, asking for what is called the action of grace; and we are asking this not only for ourselves but, as well, for those with whom we find debt. We must examine, then, other translations, which can be concluded similarly to the word debt. That which we find given here is the term binding relationship. It is not necessarily a debt; it is similar to same, but not precisely so. For one can have a relationship with another entity that, due to its nature, inhibits or limits.

In the sense of the Law called Karma, even this on the most minute level can cause this Cause and Effect Law to come into action, so to say. And so we are recognizing that even though we may not, in the conscious sense, recognize our debt, our binding relationship, our attitude which limits our effect or impact upon another, which inhibits, we are praying, "Father, in the knowledge that Thou art all, see those as we do not, and forgive us these debts, these limitations, just as we shall, and do, attempt to do as well for others." Consider this carefully. It is of much power. It is of much import.

Give us understanding, to make the right choices,
and when we fail, help us to learn from the experience.
Lead us not into temptation,
but deliver us from evil.

When one asks, Do not lead us into temptation, Father, we are asking, in essence, that which is perfect to prevent that which is imperfect, whether at the level of an action, a thing, or whatnot. Thus, we must again examine this, and we must clearly see that there is not just the implication of the literal but that which is at the deeper level. As we ask the Highest to prevent us from being limited, just in terms of the indebtedness we spoke of a moment ago above, we now ask not to be tempted. Yet we know that certain events and experiences in this or any lifetime are intentionally experienced because they afford us the opportunity for growth, for the unfoldment of wisdom.

What can this mean? How can this aspect of this prayer be of significant import that the Master might give it? We are speaking in terms also of asking to be delivered from evil. We are then to conclude by the addition of this second aspect of this phrase that we are asking that as we pass through the experience of temptation, to be guided. We are asking, lead us not into temptation, but deliver us from evil... We are asking, then, that those experiences which we are about in the Earth are not of import in and of themselves. It is that as we rise to that level of our highest within, that we can see that it is our action or reaction, how we feel about these and what we do about them.

So it is the end result, and that is the potential evil spoken of here. We are asking for wisdom. We are asking for under-standing and guidance that we shall make the choice aright. We are asking that even should we fail that we be delivered from evil in the aspects that we shall learn from this and not hold to it, not allow it to become a limitation, as well. In other words, guide us to the wisdom to see the experience for what it is and not to be tempted by it but to learn from it. And even though, Father, we pray this, should we err, give us the wisdom and the forgiveness that it shall not become evil nor a debt, a guilt, a judgment, a punishment, imposed upon self or others.

I affirm that You are all that exists
— in, about, above, below, beyond us all —
now and always.Amen.
For thine is the Kingdom
and the power and the glory
forever. Amen

We affirm, as we conclude, that Thine is the kingdom, and the power, and the glory, forever. Amen. As above, so below:

So, as we have opened with the greatest of power, we conclude with the greatest of power. We have entered this secret chamber. We have spoken our prayer, and we leave the secret chamber.

In effect, we open the door, we enter, we close it; we have our oneness with God; we reopen the door, and again, we secure it. And that prayer, that oneness with God, remains intact and holy in the sanctum sanctorum, the holiest of Holy. Our covenant with God is bound upon the table of our heart. And our highest place within has now our highest wish, our greatest hope.

We have affirmed that the Father is All... Thine is the kingdom, and that All that exists in, about, above, below, beyond us all is of the Father.

And the power... We have affirmed the power in what we have done here. And we have stated that we accept the result by stating and the glory, forever. Amen.

The Secret Chamber

This prayer, as the Master has given it, is the example. *After this manner therefore pray ye.* In other words, affirm your oneness with God, His presence within you, this being the highest and best within you. Find that place, enter into it, secure yourself therein and give unto God that which is your conscious choice, your beseechment unto God. And again, upon departing from the chamber, you secure it, you secure the thought within you

The Master spoke about the need for secrecy. He was not merely speaking this because of the obvious, that so many sought to edify themselves through their prayer, their actions or dogma, lamentations in the public square before the temple and whatnot. For they could have been as John in the wilderness, and their prayer would be heard equally, if not, indeed, more purely.

It is, then, to weaken your prayer, in essence, to take from the energy, the power, of prayer, that you shall do this in a manner which does not at the onset affirm the existence of God but rather seeks the approval of man. Are we stating that group prayer, then, is of such a nature? We of course are not. For the Master, even Himself, stated and encouraged they to gather together and pray in His name, promising that He would there be, as well. We are referring, of course, to the intent and purpose, the nature of your belief.

If one truly were to believe that it is necessary to pray in the midst of a crowd of peoples, it is possible that, at the greatest level within, there is some certain need for that entity which is fulfilled. But have a care that it is not the need to be recognized or accepted by man, lest ye place man before God.

Praying for Those Who Have "Crossed Over"

The Master very often included in this prayer that which was for those who were beyond the Earth or might be thought of (in the collective term) as dead. It is well for thee to add this to your prayer, each of you. Some state that this should be a part of the prayer. We would concur with that, though we would not in any sense change that which is holy or of significance to you.

But, as it adds to that, as it brings the greater joy, then add such as the following: And Father, we as well offer this prayer for all those souls in all realms. Or in this manner we urge you to pray. (Or, *After this manner therefore pray ye.*)

Praying for All Souls in All Realms

We would certainly include in any prayer that was stated in the plural that which would include all souls. The terminology of the prayer as it stands in its most widely accepted verbiage clearly refers primarily to the Earth. As ye would ask that the Father care for those who are beyond, you are recognizing the eternal nature of your existence. There have been those who sought to remove this from certain teachings for purposes of their own knowledge, their own intent.

Do remember to pray, as well, for those you have loved,

and yet love, who have gone before you into the other realms. For your prayer is heard there and answered there, as well.

GIVEN TO JESUS AS A SECRET TENET

The prayer was given primarily as a part of the secret tenets and/or teachings first given to the Master when He was called the man Jesus by those who were a part of the School of the Prophets as cared for, as guided those (the masters) for the teaching, He and John. And as the Expectant Ones, or Essenes, cared for, perfected, and saw to the nourishment of mind, body, and spirit, here then were these Universal Truths made known or awakened within them. Then, as the Master saw it appropriate and correct, and the need and time aright, He then gave in turn to His Disciples, as you, dear friends, in turn give to yours, your children, those whom shall follow.

The prayer was used often by the Master in His works. The prayer as given and as recorded in the mountain is recorded along with the other aspects of the Universal Law and the secret teachings, that they might be free and free others.

Again, to focus upon the chakras is to recognize the potential, the latent power, of these as aspects of self as they apply in every portion, every segment of your life… This is to make self-complete and in harmony with all existence. This is to raise the power to a point wherein the consciousness can be unified with the highest and best, the level from whence any work can be done in the Father's name.

A Prayer Oft repeated

A prayer oft repeated can be thought of from several aspects. One wherein it is used as lip service (with a note of loving humor), one is then drawn, mindfully, to certain entities of complete dedication, of complete subservience in the Eastern teachings as you know them, where prayers are not only repeated endlessly for hours, days, weeks, months, but they are written. They are changed to vibrations, ensconced in incense, in ceremony, and repeated again and again in every aspect.

It Is in the Intent

Then should we state (to answer this question) that prayers simply as a rote, as lip service, as redundant utterances, have no meaning? We believe the answer must now be clear to you, it is the intent, the purpose, the preparation, of the entity whom is in prayer that has much to do with the worthiness, so to say, the effectiveness of the prayer. You are not limited by the attitudes of others, unless you accept them as your own.

Spontaneous Prayer

The moreso a prayer is stated, the greater is its power, its strength, in the realm in which it is expressed. We do not give this that this statement then imposes a limitation on spontaneous prayer, for it is not the same. A spontaneous prayer which is not written and is of a creative nature from within self already comes from the highest and best, and is an answer to a need usually very specific and very relative to the entity who utters the prayer. There is little that can be greater than this.

Repetitive Prayer

Now we return to a prayer often and repetitively stated… It creates a vibration in the realm of its existence. That vibration, when it is repeated now by you many centuries after the prayer was initiated (by your understanding), you have the full power and presence of that prayer as a part of your statement of the prayer. Which is why so oft you will feel an energy change – an effect to your body, to your mind, to your sensory perception – when the prayer is properly stated… that is, with reverent thought and with an intent, a purpose of raising the consciousness, of affirming God's wonder, His omnipotent glory, His bond through eternity with thee.

So it is a case that we would find that depends upon self. If you think that because so many idly state this, that it hasn't the merit, then chances are it will be more difficult for you to raise your vibrations through the use of the prayer. In that instance, it might be well for you to consider others or to create one which comes from within.

Hold to the Spirit of the Prayer

Remember, *after this manner, therefore, pray ye…* You needn't cling to the precise verbiage, but do hold to the spirit, the intent. For that is what is eternal, and what shall endure. Yes, the prayer, even in the case of lip service only, still has a beneficial effect. This prayer, when spoken, produces effects on multiple levels. And if you would add an affirmation to the prayer that would recognize and include that there are, indeed, other levels, other realms, you immediately transcend them, and your prayer interconnects you with other realms.

CLOSING COMMENTS

So as you give, is it given to you: If you give to the Earth and the Earth alone, then thereof might thee think thy reward shall come. But if thee give to all of existence, then does it not follow that Universal Law would apply in a universal sensc in all of existence? Any soul in the other realms who prays and remembers all other realms, prays for you.

There are souls who are bound by aspects of limitation imposed by forces (generally, of their own acceptance) who gain greatly from a prayer such as the Lord's Prayer, as it is titled. And each time you include them (in other words, to include the dead, those who are no longer physical), each time is as a lightening of the darkness around them, until that moment when they choose to free themselves from the illusion. They shall be born swiftly and beautifully in a vehicle of pure and radiant light, composed of your prayers, and the good intents and works of those loving souls who attend to them.

You are as supplying a certain thing to other workers, and they shall weave of this supply a cloak of light which shall enable those who are held in the bondage of their own limitation to be born again freely into a greater consciousness. It is a beautiful work, one well worthy of frequent use.

Prayer Power

A prayer, when it is spoken on a certain level in a certain

realm, for example, the Earth… One might think of the Earth as a place of vibratory frequency, and that as the vibrations move away from the Earth, they become more disseminated, weaker, more rarified. But that, you see, largely depends upon the power of the entity who is in prayer.

If that entity claims their full and complete power, and acknowledges their eternal existence by including all realms in their prayer, the prayer is of such a nature that it transcends well beyond the Earth and, in effect, gains power from each realm through which it passes.

10 - Fishes and Loaves

CHANNEL/AL MINER: This is a request for a research reading titled "Fishes and Loaves." I am asked to read Mark 6, 30 to 44, which is the story of the feeding of the five thousand by Jesus.

And the apostles gathered themselves together unto Jesus, and told him all things, both what they had done, and what they had taught.

And He said unto them, Come ye yourselves apart into a desert place, and rest a while: for there were many coming and going, and they had no leisure so much as to eat.

And they departed into a desert place by ship privately. And the people saw them departing, and many knew Him, and ran afoot thither out of all cities, and out went them, and came together unto Him.

And Jesus, when He came out, saw much people, and was moved with compassion toward them, because they were as sheep not having a shepherd: and He began to teach them many things.

And when the day was now far spent, His disciples came unto Him and said, This is a desert place, and now the time is far passed:

Send them away, that they may go into the country round about, and into the villages, and buy themselves bread: for they have nothing to eat.

He answered and said unto them, Give ye them to eat. And they say unto Him, Shall we go and buy two hundred penny-worth of bread, and give them to eat?

He saith unto them, How many loaves have ye? go and see. And when they knew, they say, Five, and two fishes.

And He commanded them to make all sit down by companies upon the green grass.

And they sat down in ranks, by hundreds, and by fifties.

And when He had taken the five loaves and the two fishes, He looked up to heaven, and blessed, and brake the loaves, and gave them to his disciples to set before them; and the two fishes divided he among them all.

And they did all eat, and were filled.

And they took up twelve baskets full of the fragments, and of the fishes.

And they that did eat of the loaves were about five thousand men.

SPONSOR'S QUESTIONS

1. We ask that you would comment now on the lessons found in this miracle of abundance.

2. We ask further that you would use this story to discuss how these principles apply to our lives. Thank you.

LAMA SING COMMENTARY

There are those works which are ever governed by Forces that ye cannot see. And yet these works continue, and ye perceive them, even so, not. The way of these works is as such so as to give thee support unto thy very life.

These works are of God, truly; and, indeed, His spirit, as it walks among thee and fulfills the forces of nature and of the universe, that the way before you is aright and consistent in accordance with these laws and thy need.

It is oft given here that the Light is upon thee once again. Some of thee who hear know that we speak of Him who has come unto thee in past.

Those who can see shall soon know even moreso than that of which we speak.

BY AFFIRMATION THE POWER IS INVOKED

Within the Law, we have spoken in past regarding that called the Word, the Word of God. The Word is the action, and here we find that the thought is expressed not in a sense verbally, but rather by the thought or the word given in prayer. By affirmation, the power is, in essence, invoked. The Master, in prayer, places Himself within that flow of energy, and abideth by that Law Universal, and thus makes His will at one with the Father's. Thusly so can He command all forces in the name of the Father, and thusly so do we find the Father's Will expressed in His every action and deed.

Herein, then, is there the Law of God expressed through the alignment of self with those Forces spiritual and eternal. Some would call the force of nature (which is, even so, to say the Spirit of God), and others would say the Universal Forces and, even further, by other titles and names do yet others call these. And so it is not unto the word as can be called upon this as an action, as a force, as a deed, but rather that the word given is intended to create a thought, a form, a spiritual understanding.

The Word of God Is the Fulfillment

And so, the Word of God is the action, the movement, the need, and the fulfillment of the need. Here then find that the Master has called apart, first of all, His brethren... His followers, the Disciples. He knew, of their hearts and minds, many teachings that they had done, and many works did they, as well, in His name.

As He perceived them, He knew further that each did have this or that question, doubt, apprehension, fear, or whatnot. In the wisdom of God within Him, He then took them unto a distant place, knowing that therein could He give the answer to each question within the heart of all of these entities, through the activities or the actions of a single deed; and, to that extent, as might give rise to a better understanding, through the performance of the living example and, through this, give hope and promise to the flocks which would follow.

Commanding the Word

As substance in the Earth is gathered up and placed in the hands of the Master, it matters not whether these be fishes or loaves, it matters not whether these be waters of a great sea or stones of which a mountain is constructed. For in His moments of oneness with God and His application of the Law Universal, He commanded the Word of God in the lands of man. In His hand, a simple loaf required no great work, no great effort, but only the open palms of His up-stretched hands to show unto the Force eternal that which was needed, with no anxiety, without doubt, fear, or concerns of any lot.

For, what Force has given this loaf into the hands of a man? Is it borne within a tiny seed? Surely one seed cannot contain such a loaf. Is it bound in the nature of many seeds? While truly that which is the potential for the loaf can be said to be found within a quantity of these grains, there must be the action of the grinding, and there must be the activity which has caused the growth of these seeds in the earlier steps. And there must be the separation of the fruit from the chaff. And there must be the drying. There must be the preparation and the blending of these fruits of the grain unto other elements and the subjection of these unto the heat, the oven. And there must be that which gives way, then, in order that all this might be done and finally come unto this place and be in this man's hands, now up-stretched unto His Father.

Commanding the Universal Forces

So then, did man place this loaf in His hands, the Master's hands? In a manner, a man giveth this unto Jesus. Of course, dear friends, thou knoweth that this cometh from God, from the Force Universal, and that the nature force, which is as the Spirit Yahweh or God, has given the energies, the vibrations, the forces, the nutrients, the rays, the sun, all of which were required to bring this loaf unto the hands of the Master.

Then if one is in alliance or in harmony with that Force

Universal, is it required that more be present than this to bring other loaves into existence? Are the Forces which gave rise to this loaf not present? Is the bearer of the loaf, the one whom has the need and seeks the loaf, is He not, as well, present?

GOD ANSWERS EVERY PRAYER

So we have, then, the source and need, not so as to mock God or to tempt Him, but to come unto God with a need and to place self in harmony with the Spirit of God, so that there might be the passing through of His Will and the completeness of the answer to this and every prayer. So as these hands, then, returned into the sphere of the Earth from the heavens into which they were thrust, the hands did multiply the loaves; and the loaves did multiply unto themselves; and for as many as there were in need, the loaves they did multiply.

And of the great sea came the fishes; and the fishes into the hands of the Master, upraised, and into the Spirit of God. The symbol of this fish, simple and nourishing to spirit and to body, the Son of Man did envision in prayer the Law of God which is as Abundance. As He returned, then, His consciousness and this fish into the sphere of the Earth, and did into the baskets thrust same, He did multiply them; and they did multiply unto the need of those who were present.

Degrees of Faithfulness

Each of you, then, will look upon this with a varying reaction, a varying degree of faithfulness.

There may be those among you who will be in askance: Be this truth or mere folk tale? And yet others will say: It is possible for such an entity to so do, but for I it is unlikely.

And there will be certain among ye who will believe. And unto these, we say these words: O, ye who are faithful, unto ye it shall be given in accordance with thy need. And if ye ask of the Father, ask in thy nature of eternal being and it shall be, unto thee, given in accordance with thy need and the need of those whom thee seek to serve in His name. Neither shall thee doubt nor question nor give rise to those attitudes which would limit. For these Forces are of the most gracious and most loving, and shall enter into that realm wherein there is peace and there, invitation. As ye doubt, ye bolt the chamber of thine own abundance. Where there is faith, the latch is loosened and the portal is opened, that abundance can flow forth.

As the Disciples did see and witness this, there was a realization, an answer, if you will, unique to the individual needs of each entity. And where, heretofore, there had gone question or doubt, there was replaced a certain inner understanding. And so a portal of great value was opened within them, and this they would, each one, use in the Earth days beyond.

So accustomed unto the Master's love and compassion and His works of wonder had they become, that unto these actions they gave no great note, save within their hearts. For they were heavy with their own deeds and burdened with their own works, which they had performed in His name. They did rise upon this occurrence and did become much moreso hardened unto the Way, and unto that which lay ahead.

Thou might thinketh: How be it that there is given that the Disciples are hardened by this action? Consider, then, that there was the need of these peoples. Consider, then, that the Master fulfilled the need. If they had, in the teachings and in the wisdom imparted unto them by the Master in past, truly accepted His word, could they not, even each one, fulfill the needs of the hungered?

Is it greater for a man to feed his brother who is hungered of body than it is to feed a hungry spirit? Is it greater to give rest to a weary and troubled mind and heart, than it is to give up thy bed chamber to a weary body? Which then is the greater? The gift of wealth unto one whom is in need or the gift of prayer? We know that your minds will answer in a certain manner. We know that in your hearts you will think in certain other ways. And we also know that in your spirit you see truth. We do not answer the questions we just gave unto thee, for it is for each one of thee to answer them.

All Are Given According to The Need

We do state these things in humbleness: If thou art a servant of God, and His way and thine are bound unto oneness, and if in the course of traveling His way, thee find need and thou art asked in His name to fill that need, this ye can do and this the Father would have thee do. But if there is found in the heart of the one who is asking of thee some certain thing which prevents the fulfillment of the request, then has God abandoned thee, or the one who seeks from thee?

We say unto thee, none are abandoned, but all are given that which they need. If thou needeth to see the fulfillment of the requestor's needs, thou art wanting in thy spirit. If the seeker needs fulfillment, and seeks from thee and of God because they shall not tend to their own path, then they are of idle heart in their seeking. But if the seeker has given and has learned and is open in the heart, unto these shall it be given.

Ask from an Open Heart

If thou art His disciple and thou seek to fulfill only for the joy of fulfillment and because it is thy work to serve His Will, then through thee it shall be given. Wherever a temple is builded upon a man, that temple shall not endure; wherever a temple is builded within a man, that temple dwelleth throughout eternity, for man is eternal within.

Seek of That Within, Not That Without

If, upon the pathway of life now before thee, there is found one who is hungered, shall thee go forth to them and offer food? Yes, for all are hungered, and the food is the letter and Word of the Law, for all are hungered of spirit, and all are in need. Make, then, that nourishment for their spirit open unto them. But just so as their spirit seeth not from the body, so doth the food which thou give unto them likewise not appear. If they look with their spirit, they shall see the bounty which you offer them. If they look with the eyes of their body, they shall see naught, and the way shall continue.

Seek from the Spirit

So is it written then, if ye seek, it shall be given unto thee. Ye must seek of spirit, not of body, for body is the product of the spirit. The tool does not do the work unless the worker recognizes it. There is not the idle worker and the active tool.

So if ye seek in your lives – each one, dear friends – to fulfill a need, then see the need in the eyes of your spirit. Be certain that it is a need, as opposed to the potential of it being an opportunity. For if we take an entity's opportunity, we've taken from them the nourishment of their body spiritual, and they shall grow weaker. This we must not do, for this, you see, moves against the Law Universal.

But as we see their need, and look unto it with the eye of spirit and we see that it is opportunity, we need not turn away from the call, for we are those who seek to feed His flock. Let us then feed this entity in need by giving the information which will help the entity to see this in its rightful light as a gift, an opportunity, given from his loving father.

CLOSING COMMENTS

How does the spirit weaken itself? We have just given one method. Wherein an opportunity is removed, then the food for the spirit is taken from that entity.

And how might we create in accordance with the Law of Abundance and the miracle of the fishes and loaves? How might we give and fulfill in the multiplication through the Law of Abundance? We have given, just above, that we must look from the spiritual sight. We see the need. We discern it. We open self as an instrument of the Universal Forces of God, and we give that which we have to give. We give of our wisdom, our knowledge, our experience. But more importantly, we give of our spirit and of our love. For the moreso we can give of these, the moreso are they multiplied within us.

If we give unto you a loving thought, the Father replaces it within us many-fold over. If you take unto this and break it as a loaf into many pieces, and give it unto those who are hungered, dost thou not then multiply further in accordance with the Law of Abundance? Dost thou not, then, function, even so, as the Christ, Himself, as He now stands before thee, offering thee a loaf? Wilt thou not take this loaf and break it and give it unto those who are hungered? Wilt thou not multiply this within thine own being, that it might pour forth from thee as the nourishing rain of spirit upon a land which is parched?

Ye have asked of us: How be it this miracle applies unto our lives? We have given it, and it is our prayer that ye have heard it. For as ye use that which thee have, the Father giveth unto thee many-fold over to replace it.

11 - Jesus Walks on Water

CHANNEL/AL MINER: This reading is a request for a research reading on the story of Jesus' walking on the water as is told in Matthew 14, verses 22 to 33, which I will now read:

And straightway Jesus constrained his disciples to get into a ship, and to go before him unto the other side, while he sent the multitudes away.

And when he had sent the multitudes away, he went up into a mountain apart to pray: and when the evening was come, he was there alone. But the ship was now in the midst of the sea, tossed with waves: for the wind was contrary.

And in the fourth watch of the night Jesus went unto them, walking on the sea.

And when the disciples saw him walking on the sea, they were troubled, saying, It is a spirit; and they cried out for fear.

But straightway Jesus spake unto them, saying, Be of good cheer; it is I; be not afraid.

And Peter answered him and said, Lord, if it be thou, bid me come unto thee on the water.

And he said, Come. And when Peter was come down out of the ship, he walked on the water, to go to Jesus.

But when he saw the wind boisterous, he was afraid; and beginning to sink, he cried, saying, Lord, save me.

And immediately Jesus stretched forth his hand, and caught him, and said unto him, O thou of little faith, wherefore didst thou doubt?

And when they were come into the ship, the wind ceased. Then they that were in the ship came and worshipped him, saying, Of a truth, thou art the Son of God.

SPONSOR'S QUESTIONS

1. We ask now that we might receive a commentary on the lessons found in this miracle of nature.

2. Please use this story to discuss the principles that Jesus used here and how they apply to our lives.

LAMA SING COMMENTARY

There is much which can be gained through the study of that as given above, but not so much so as one would labor over this or that word or phrase, but rather in a manner which, by allowing self to hear with the spirit, the soul, one would be awakened in a sort of understanding which would be unique unto self; and which, by its nature, would contribute unto the understanding of thy individual pathway. So, that which is awakened by the narrative above… may it be a lamp for you and a light for others.

THE MASTER WAS A MASTER

Understand that the Master was, indeed, a master, having the knowledge both through the evolvement of His soul (His spiritual life force), by His early choice (that is, in that portion of the soul journey which is called early defined by a linear progression of your time understanding). He did choose at this time through His awareness to follow this certain pathway of evolvement.

Then too (with John and the others) lovingly and wisely trained, not so much so as to instill knowledge but to awaken it. And then in the evolvement, through the sharing and the affirmations as were His testings, His opportunities – no different, dear friends, than your own individual opportunities or challenges in life – He became, indeed, a master, as implied by this term or title, one who could command, one who had mastery over the forces of His domain (that, then, being the Earth itself and its surrounding realms and more, to be sure, but sufficient unto the needs of the present is the description as above).

One Who Could Command

He was, further, by the interpretation of this title, one who could lead and could command. So then, elemental forces were within His ability to command. His connective link with the eternal Source, which is God, was clear and unobstructed. His works were as exercises to strengthen even moreso this bond, this conductive link, between His Earthly consciousness and His soul consciousness at one with God.

THE LESSON

Contributed His Knowledge to His Followers

He did then choose varying incidents, varying situations, wherein He could contribute this knowledge as a form of training, as a type of initiation, unto His followers. And by using the elemental forces of the kingdom of Earth (as it might be called), He did give unto them brilliantly and lovingly the tools with which they might therein and henceforth do works in the Father's name.

He Created a Temporary Separateness

So we find at the onset of the narrative, the Master bids them to depart, creating a temporary separateness. You will note in the annals of recorded history, this is normal, this is the logical choice at varying points between a master and initiates.

Raised Himself Above Mass-Thought

He did then complete His works and selected an opportunity and a locale wherein (and you will note) He was able to bring His physical body to a significant height above mass-thought, above a sort of radionic force which is more dense and, thus, more intense in the lower lands.

Entered into a State of Oneness

Rising to the summit and sequestering Himself, He did enter into a state of oneness, only after assuring that all conditions, as were able to so be controlled, were controlled. He entered into that still, small place, as close as He could move physically, mentally, and then spiritually through prayer. Mentally, yes.

He separated Himself by physical distance from His Disciples, knowing that their mind-forces would thusly consider that they were apart and their thoughts would not be reaching out quite so strongly unto Him. The highland aided this and so forth, you see, much in the manner as the information we have given oft-times in past to many of thee.

Released His Consciousness, Received the Spirit

As He prayed, He did release the last vestiges of His own consciousness and in-filled Himself with the eternal Spirit. In this, then, He did perceive His works and He did perceive His Disciples. In the building of those forces which then created the awareness, the awaken-ness, of the Disciples, the Master gained their attention and, in a sense, created the most profound of environs possible in that instance wherein they might learn. Whereupon, as they reached that moment of great fear, He did move Himself within a distance of their vessel and then commenced to walk upon the water.

Their awareness perceived Him and doubted, and only after Peter went forth and, through his fear, fell and was lifted up by the Master and subsequently their entry into the vessel, did the others truly believe the Master was, in truth, physically present. And so, you see, their belief was instilled firmly and with a manner that would not be forgotten by them or all who would hear the words and know in spirit this to be of truth.

APPLY THE PRINCIPLES

There are many valuable lessons in this, dear friends. First of all, understand by listening and seeing.

Control and Rise Above the Conditions

The Master controlled, first, the environ. He used His mental and physical body to make conditions aright to the best of His ability and to the fullness of measure. Then moving, as a part of that control, to a high place, He freed His mind, allowing His spiritual force to enter and to, in effect, make His body, His mind, and His spirit as one. He was thusly and in that instant in harmony with all forces, presenting no challenge, no issue of harm, only love, only harmony. and tranquility.

Then, as you, dear friend, would seek to be a disciple, to be an initiate, learn from this. Can thee control certain habits, certain doubts? Art thou able to do as the Master and rise above, if not in the literal sense, in the sense of separating self from those areas of great influence that these might not be, in any sense, a limitation unto you, and that the vestiges which might otherwise bind thee would be loosed and thou would be, in that essence, free? Then, even so as thy body might be in residence apart from those things familiar, apart from those things which draw upon thee in this way or that, thee must now release the thought.

Remove Self from the Familiar

Again, oft-times distance in the physical or geographical sense has an impact here, for it is the thought-form or impression of others that can very often cause them and self to consider that thou art beyond the mental-emotional influence. (We must add here, this is not accurate, but it is the way of thinking in Earth at present and, thus, its impact, its influence, is sufficiently effective, do you see. There is some humor here regarding this, indeed.)

Enter into Silence

And then it becomes the matter of entering into silence, symbolized by nightfall when the Earth becomes at rest. And when the masses, the peoples, are in a state of repose, their mental forces, their emotive energy, is attuned to the Universal Force in the state you call sleep, those Forces which are eternally creative are unencumbered and, in essence, available for those who might use them in great plentitude. You see from this so much that you can do, so much that you can contribute to making the way easier. But what shall occur from this point forward, and what were the Principles as applied by the Master? These, again, are quite clear.

Return the Spiritual Force to the Body and Mind

Entering into this state, observing now the methodical care, the logic, the wisdom, applied by the Master without effort to bring Himself to this point of the highest and best receptivity, He entered into His spirit and returned His spiritual force unto His body and mind.

Command the Creative Force

Thou knoweth that the Spirit is that which creates all things; and if the Creative Force is the primal force or thought-form within thee, then thou art a creative force in and of yourself. As such, you can move at will and in harmony with all things, for thou art of that substance of which they are in existence. Your body is intact in its physical understanding; it is not affected by the laws of Earth but is, in effect, in harmony and in mastery of them. An example of this is the force called gravity. This is, in essence, a type of magnetic force (as you think of it), but it is moreso a force of agreement. That is to say that all consciousness that dwells and interacts within the sphere of the Earth, in the dimension which you recognize as Earth, agrees that the Earth has its axis and its polarity, and so it does. And there is agreement that this force is that which is needed to conform to the laws which are intended for the progression of the souls thereupon, also agreed upon.

As you move into this vein of thought, you will begin to feel a curious sense of freedom. First, it will come to you as an instant of insight and then may not reappear for several repeated attempts. But with perseverance it will return again, and this time for a longer period, perhaps two or three seconds, your time measure, and then not return again. But this time, its next return will be sooner. There will be less time between its occurrence. Again and again, until it can be summoned with relative ease, and, with concentration and familiarity and acceptance, can be sustained for prolonged periods of time.

Free Self from the Forces That Bind

What occurs therein, within the body and this activity, is that, once the Law is understood and once one realizes that their individual agreement is the true force that binds them to the laws of the Earth, they are suddenly freed.

The first stages will be movement as a thought or thought-form, or as a spiritual consciousness. Then there will come sustained movement, wherein you may be perceived here or there (or felt, at least), and so on and so forth, until such time as thee would actually move from one physical location in Earth to another. See? Even so as we have spoken these words just passed unto you, dear friend, a portion of your consciousness wishes to believe this to be true. Another portion of your being tells you that, of course, it must be true. And yet another aspect questions, doubts, and even denies it as a possibility:

Even if this is possible, for example, for one such as the Master could it be possible for thee? And could this be possible now, in this lifetime? Perhaps next year? Even in the next month? Or tomorrow? Could it be possible within the next hour? Is it possible now? Of course it is, dear friends. The separateness is, as Peter showing that he had faith and that he had learned much from the Master as an adept, as a Disciple; but when confronted with the challenge on the part of the forces (which, mind thee, were stirred by the Master Himself) Peter did fear and did doubt, and his harmony with the forces gave way to his acceptance of the law, the rule, the condition, the illusion, of the Earth.

But even so, as he had begun to sink, he called out unto the Master, for his faith in the Master was profound. The instantaneous touch of the Master's hand upon his did not lift him from the water, but gave him the strength and the balance to rise up instantly of his own accord. It was not the Master's physical force which pulled him from the water, but his belief in the Master's powers that caused him to move immediately into a renewed state of harmony with those forces of nature, those Forces Universal.

APPLYING THE TOOLS TODAY

Where do you begin? Begin where thou art. What are the tools? The tools are those things which are before thee in thy life at this moment. Dost thou not see them? Then look through our eyes, dear friend, as we lovingly and humbly attempt to assist thee.

The Time of Greatest Harmony: Twilight

The sun shall rise in the heaven of thy Earth on the morrow, and thee shall (for the most part) rise as well. Why do you not rise when the sun sets, for therein lies the time of greatest harmony and greatest peace in the mental and emotional spheres abounding in and about Earth? You do so in this manner because it is the nature of man, and it is agreed upon by all (except as ye might be called to work in the eveningtide).

Ye consider the light of the sun in a manner synonymous with the Light of God. Yet is not God present irrespective of the light of a single sphere in the heavens of the Earth? Certainly. Each of thee know the joy and blessing of prayer in the quiet hours of early morn or late evening or night.

Did thee note that it was the fourth watch of the night wherein the Master chose to do these works and give these great lessons unto His children? We find this to be approximately three to four hours past midnight, do you see, a time which we have suggested often to many of you as profound, in terms of receptiveness for meditation. So this, then, is a tool. Now that thee know of it, thee might use it.

Release Judgment of Self and Others

Begin by applying truth in your daily life. Is there not one or more entities in the Earth about whom thee have thoughts of anger, of doubt, of remorse, of fear, of guilt, of jealousy? Work upon these. These are your tools. If ye can overcome this, then you will loose a bond which is secured firmly to you and preventing you from being free.

Is there some judgment you have placed upon yourself for

having done some certain thing, or perhaps not having done some certain thing? Curious is it not? Then loose this bond. Do what must be done to understand that such attitudes of guilt or self-judgment serve not but, rather, bind.

Free Self from Habit

Is there that in your life present which is unpleasant for thee as a task? There, too, is a tool. Discover why. Have you bound yourself to this task errantly? Is this something in which thee have no belief or faith and yet ye perpetuate because it seems it must be done? Free yourself from this.

Develop a Christly Attitude Towards Abundance

Art thou of great wealth in the Earth? Dost thee possess many things of physical nature? Do these bring thee joy? If so, that is good, and that is the application of our Father's Law.

Do thee have a bond to these things, or are they held loosely in the openness of thy hands as precious and gentle gifts from a loving Father, but not clung to in a manner which burdens thee or weights thee? Art thou poor in terms of these things? Is there a great desire for things of the Earth? If so, then thou art as burdened by this desire as that entity of wealth in Earth may be burdened by a certain obsession to obtain more and to possess and to cling.

So it is not, see, a burden to have gifts or abundance in the Earth. It is the attitude and the reaction to these. They are gifts and tools no different than the woodworker's carving implements. It is what the skill and the heart of the woodworker brings unto his tools that shall create and fashion a work of beauty. Then look into thy life's heart and see these things as we have given them and all those others which are of such import to thee as that they burden and as that they suppress the lightness of heart and the gladness of spirit.

There are many in distant lands (to each of you, distant) who have discarded all such things, all such associations, all such possessions, and are still not free. How can this be? For they have only abandoned them. They have not given up their desire for them. In the abandonment, for many, the desire is increased. It is not necessary that thee deny all things in the Earth, but deny their bond upon you. Very often this cannot be separated in entities in Earth, and they must do both in order to accomplish the one, the freeing of self.

As the Master told one to Go, and give away all that thou hast, the entity could not do so. So then, that which he had, possessed him. But unto another, He spoke these same or similar words, and the entity joyously did so, and was freed. But he was not freed because he gave away that which he had; he was freed because he was able to so do. His riches, his bounty, were within, and all things were brought unto him. And he became a great king and became known for his wisdom all throughout many lands.

Unburden Self from All That Binds

So, within each of thee there is the potential and, indeed, the ability, the wisdom, and knowledge, to make self light, unburdened by any such doubt, fear, guilt, judgment, or what-not as might burden thee. Remember, mind is the builder. And mind so oft builds from emotion, as the substance, the force, or energy, from which mind can build in the physical.

Water: The Symbol of the Life-Force of God

Water is the symbol of spirit. It is the symbol of God. If one is at one with his Father, would they not, first and above all, find total harmony with water? Water is present both symbolically and literally in nearly all things in the Earth (indeed, we are advised, in all things to an extent or another). So if one is in harmony, in a state of oneness, with water – that is Spirit – are they not to the greater or lesser degree instantly in harmony with all things?

If thee command an entity to be healed in the name of the Christ, dost thou not speak to their spirit? Dost thou not speak to their waters of life? Then think thou often of water as the very life-force of God, that the symbology of this would be borne ever in mind. Water is transmutable. It is a substance, a force, an energy, which can adapt to any form of expression, whether solid, liquid, or gaseous. It can move freely and without effort. It always seeks its own, its source.

So much to be learned, and so much to be borne, ever, as a guiding wisdom if one considers Spirit as water. In each lesson, in each wisdom, given by a master, there is a certain symbol, some certain phrases and that sort, which can be used as keys to sustain a consciousness and to retain and be able to quickly apply a truth or a law.

If thee seek, then, to command and be at one with the forces of thy sphere, think thou of water. If thee seek, then, to be in harmony with all things and to give life and love unto them, think thou of water.

If an entity is injured, you soothe them with healing waters. Then when in meditation or prayer for another, see waters of light cascading down over the entity in need, swirling about them, penetrating every fiber of their being. Speak to the waters of each cell. Call them out if they are errant, and purify the waters, displacing the dross and the illusion.

If there is one whose body is withered, restore it by replenishing the waters of their fiber, of their mind and heart, and of their spirit.

If a traveler, wearied by his journey, should behold thee and ask thee for a cup of water, thou would surely give this unto him, would thee not? How be it, then, that thou perceiveth an entity who is in a state of disease different than a weary traveler? They ask of thee for the cup of water. Can thee do less than give this unto them?

CLOSING COMMENTS

The moreso a rivulet within thee is used, the greater and deeper shall its channel become; the moreso the waters of spirit pour through thee, the closer ye shall find self moving unto its Source. And if thee and the waters of eternal life become as one in works of joy and light to the Father's name, wilt they not ever support thee and know thee to be their own?

Ponder in thy secret place these words, for they are words of truth, and we give them unto thee now that they shall set thee free. If thee know of this, thee know of all things.

If thee have the wisdom of what is now spoken unto thee, thou art at one with our Father's Spirit. We pray that it be written so upon the tables of thine heart and be bound to thee throughout eternity as kinsmen.

We thank thee in humble joy for this opportunity to have been with thee once again. (And we thank those loving souls who seek this information in the name of the Christ and to be given as a light unto others. Unto you, we ask at this time a light of spiritual water to be given unto your soul as a cup of loving nourishment from your brethren here unto one of our own in the realm of Earth.) And this too, dear friends, we share with each of you.

12 - *Jesus Heals – Part 2*

CHANNEL/AL MINER: This is a request for a topical research reading, the title of which is Jesus Heals - Part II. I would like to thank the sponsor of this beautiful work. I think it's appropriate that we are requesting this reading just a couple weeks before we celebrate the entry of the Master once again. They write as follows:

SPONSOR'S QUESTIONS:

Dear Lama Sing: Here are three more stories of healings by Jesus. One reason these are being presented is that we would like to be able to do the works of Jesus. We are hoping that, by giving you several readings on this topic, you might take different approaches, one of which might "click" with us and give us the insight to do these works.

(And I'll mention again that this is the third and last of this series, the first being Lazarus [which appears in Book Two] and Jesus Heals - Part I, and now this one, Part II.)

1. In the story of the healing of the child from Mark 9, why did the Disciples have difficulty, and what did Jesus do that overcame this? What did He mean by *This kind can come out by nothing, save by prayer?* Or *prayer and fasting as some authorities have it?*

(And for your reference, this is Mark 9, verses 17-29. And there are some beautiful quotes in here, ones that I'd like to insert here. I won't read the whole thing because it's lengthy.

And Jesus said unto him, If thou canst believe, all things are possible to him that believeth.

And then straightaway the father of the child cried out and said, I believe. Help thou mine unbelief.

And then Jesus rebuked the unclean spirit and said, I

command thee, come out of him. And then Jesus took the child by the hand and raised him up.

2. In the story of the blind man at Bethesda, Jesus seemed to have performed the healing twice to get completion of the process. He also used spittle in this instance, and finally He told this man not to enter into the village. Would you comment on these, please? (That is Mark 8: 22-26)

3. In the story of the Gadarene demoniac, please explain who or what the devils were. How would we know that they are present in modern times? How does one drive out devils like this?

(This is from, I believe, from Luke, Chapter 8, verses 26-39. This is where the devils entered the swine, you may recall. Very lengthy but very beautiful, fascinating discourse.)

4. Why were some who were healed told to declare how great things were done for them by God, and others were told to tell no man? In Luke 26-39, verse 39 says, *Return to thy house and declare how great things God hath done for thee.*

5. In the story of the Syro-Phoenician woman, the verbal interchange between her and Jesus is a little disturbing, in that it implies that she is among the dogs. It seems harsh and out of character for Jesus.

(This would be Matthew, Chapter 15, versus 22-28. This is very interesting. I'm going to read this; it's brief.)

And behold, a Canaanitish woman came out from those borders and cried, saying, Have mercy on me, O Lord, thou son of David. My daughter is grievously vexed with the devil.

But He answered her not a word, and His Disciples came and besought Him, saying, Send her away, for she crieth after us.

But He answered and said, I was not sent but unto the lost sheep of the house of Israel.

But she came and worshipped Him, saying, Lord, help me,

And He answered and said, It is not meet to take the chil-

dren's bread and cast it to the dogs.

But she said, Yea, Lord, for even the dogs eat of the crumbs which fall from their masters' table.

Then Jesus answered and said unto her, O woman, great is thy faith. Be it done unto thee, even as thou wilt. And her daughter was healed from that hour."

As in all these stories, there are undoubtedly subtleties that we don't understand. Please feel free to discuss these and any other topics that you judge to be important or interesting to us. Thank you, Al and Lama Sing. Blessings.

LAMA SING COMMENTARY

There is much, dear friends, in the questions and examples given above, which can be of inspiration and guidance to you. In these collective works performed in this meeting, we shall, in humbleness, in gratitude to the Master for this opportunity, offer to you these insights as they are given to us here from consciousness universal.

THE MASTER TAUGHT

Those who followed, who walked with, the Master, who heard His teachings repeatedly, and of course, those who were chosen to be of the inner circle of light around the Master, were sent forth to do various works of a healing nature. In the process of these works, the Master's wisdom and higher sight perceived that, they would be challenged and gifted with the opportunities of this or that situation, which would bring forth the greater brilliance of their individual spirits from within.

Prayer and Fasting

And so, as in this first example, as they told the Master that they were unable to do this work, and questioned mysteriously why this might be so, the Master points out here in the comment about the need for prayer and fasting in such works that here there is a powerful, we could call it, thought-form or intention, which is very much native to the Earth. So that even those of the Disciples, whose continual presence with the Master should have brought them to a position of loving neutrality, or such a state so as to be unaffected by forces of the Earth, were still challenged.

Thought-Forms Associated with Earth

So the Master's teaching here was to them: Look within yourselves in prayer, in meditation; see what aspects of self are still vulnerable to the native forces of the Earth; then, as needs be, fast. For as you take in the fruits of the earth, there are thought-forms, there are essences, associated with same. While even those nourish the body, they can and ofttimes do contain certain energies or thought-forms that can limit.

The 'Devil': That Which Deters or Limits

How? Limit by making the way passable into the practitioner, so that the limitation of the one in need – the subject, the patient, the target of your work – can use this to diminish the power, the omnipotence, of your faith. These are called here devil. In the sense of the several-fold interpretations of these, the Aramaic, the Greek, the Hebraic, there are variants. We could look to defining this, for sake of reference in this work, as that which deters you, that which limits you, and that which has a residual impact upon your habits, your attitudes, your emotions. In other words, the devil is that which keeps the status quo. See?

Disease and Dis-Ease

Now, in some instances, as in the examples given above, these have also predicated significant conditions of dis-ease (remembering that disease and dis-ease are one and the same). So that illnesses, sickness, infirmities, disfiguration, limitations of all sort, are conditions, first and foremost, of a lack of ease in spirit, mind, emotion, and then predicated or precipitated into the physical body.

Becoming Neutral, or Centered

So the Master here is urging the entities who are practitioners, his Disciples, that they must, even moreso, center themselves, focus themselves, so as to become so neutral that the grace of God can flow through them and manifest its love, its forgiveness, its faith, and its purity, so as to promote a state of ease. Reminding you again that the Master oft went apart from the populace, even from the Disciples, to pray, to fast, to meditate. Even from His position as the Christ in the form of the man called Jesus, was He very aware that even subtleties of thought, of emotive energy in the Earth, can accumulate. Not within Him but, perhaps, as He saw it, about Him. Sort of like a spiritual venting, if you will.

In the casting out (as the phrase is given in the examples above is manifested), first, you, as practitioners, should center yourself. What do we mean by this? Find a state of joyful ease, a position of balance, a neutrality, a state of loving neutrality, which begins with the claiming of one's own love within, for self, for the God within, for the Christ spirit within, and for the pathway of service that is before you.

Seeking a State of Empowerment

Once this is done, then a state of empowerment should be sought after. Recognizing that you are a Child of God, that you are eternal, that you are, therefore, a part of God, and no part of God is without God's power, God's grace and love. Rising, even if but for a few minutes, to a place of authority, a place of righteousness, where you can turn to the person in need, whether they are physically present or nay, and command.

ON HEALING

Asking on Behalf of Another

In these examples, there are several instances where the entities could not ask for themselves. Knowing that Free Will is very important, if not pivotal, in manifesting Universal Law, God's Law, the question here, then, might arise, "How is it possible to heal one who cannot ask, or will not ask, or knows not to seek?" There is a connection between those who are asking on behalf of the dis-eased. That connection is a path of light that is, in the Earthly sense, due to their relationship in the parental sense, or in other instances, as well. Example: where one asks for healing for their servant. (Remember?)

Connecting Through the Line of Light

This spirit of connection of life, the line of light or life between these entities, is sort of a manifestation of another facet of Free Will. Because there is this bond, paternal bond, then the inability of the entity, because they have subjugated their will somehow, in one way or another, enables, empowers, brings to the forefront, the positive side of Universal Law, even that of Free Will.

There is another way to build this bridge of light, and that is through true, pure, spiritual love, where you can look at the entity in need and feel a sense of connectedness, where you can reach out with your mind and spirit and know this entity to be in need, and know them to be unable to speak, asking for assistance. You are, in effect, bypassing the physical manifestation of that entity, and making a connection with their spirit self. You will know, probably by some reaction to the body which is stimulating to the neurological, to the musculature, or by a pulsing in the body, an electrical feeling, or a reaction very powerful at the solar plexi center.

Any or all of these may occur. This is a clear indicator to you, in terms of giving you (what you would call) the green light to go ahead. It's almost unmistakable. Once you have experienced it, you will never forget it. This connection is very empowering, but to know it, to claim it, one must be very focused, very centered, very open. And that is the reason why the Master's answer was and is as given: "These can come out only by prayer and fasting, by meditation," and focus. See?

Understanding Habit

The habits, the powers of habit, are fueled by the Forces which could be called shadowy, limiting. How is this possible without an identity, an entity, a devil? It is very simple. It is possible because many entities who are participating in that (we'll call it) mass-mind thought-form are interacting with it continually. It is like a massive chorus, where many voices come together to create a secondary sound which, for the most part, is heard as a collage of sound, rather than a single voice. So, with the shadowy Forces of habit and limitation (and not all habits are limiting, but can be, see), as with these, then, the thoughts and the desires of those who are a part of that particular type of shadowy thought-form are continually fueling all of those who are a part of it.

In the instance of those who are dis-eased, this dis-ease is because of a collective way of thinking or habit. Collective, from where (for some are children)? Obviously, from past lives and previous incarnations, in other realms, in other dimensions, as well as the Earth. These are points of powerful potential for these souls. So powerful, that they manifest in a way which is outstandingly unique. Not just a withered limb, lost sight, diminished hearing, a dis-ease to the digestive, or on and on; but the total (seemingly, at least) subjugation of their conscious will to the shadowy Forces. See?

The Nature of Dis-Ease

When there are those conditions of dis-ease and/or limitation which have become so familiar to the one who is dis-eased, a sort of spiritual, mental, and emotional callus forms. Remember your physical bodies. If you do a certain work that causes abrasion, pressure, continual stress or duress upon some part of the body – let's say the hands, for example, for that's the most common – then the body responds by building up reserve tissues. It builds layer upon layer, to form a callus. The skin hardens, toughens, and is more tolerant of the continual challenge made to it.

As above, so is it below; as below, so is it above: the spirit, then, under a continual duress, the emotion battered continually by the same Forces, builds a callus and becomes more and more oblivious to those Forces, so that they can take a sort of semi-permanent residency in that person's life. The callus actually becomes a part of the perpetuation of the dis-ease. Now, remember, we are speaking here of a protective mechanism to the emotion, to the mind, to the heart. And so, the condition of limitation manifests in the physical body. See?

Finding the Entry-Point of the Dis-Ease

So the Master, or you, can look for this. Where is the tolerance? Where is the entry point, that this dis-ease has found its way into the physical body? You might be able to see it in the energy fields around the physical body, if you have allowed yourself the higher sight. Notice the wording: if you have allowed yourself higher sight.

When we use the word see, we are not referring to physical sight; we are referring (humbly and lovingly) to all sight, which can include, of course, the literal seeing of the aura, the energy fields, and such. But perhaps even more important is the capacity to feel it, to know it, and to do so to such an affinity, without claiming it, without sharing in it, that you can not only identify it, but take command over it.

The Forces That Limit and Loving Neutrality

These Forces know the Light very well. And they will know of your coming and your intention, even – notice this – even before you do. They know of the intention of the host, the entity who is dis-eased by their presence, who is about to seek healing. They will fortify in any way possible in advance of that request. They will put forth buffers, veils, things to confuse you, to mislead you, all manner of such, for the Earth is where they dwell.

God and God's Spirit is life and the foundation upon which the Earth rests. But God's Spirit is the epitome of loving neutrality, a father-mother who knows that their children learn through doing, through experiencing, through interacting. It is so beautiful, so wonderful. And when you know it and claim it, then you will see these deceptions, these veils, these buffers, these illusions that the shadowy Forces try to impart.

Karma

Remember, they are very familiar with the Earth. It is who and what they are. It is their realm of expression. These shadowy Forces cannot move up to the higher realms. And this creates the Sea of Faces, the limited realms beyond the finite, the incarnate expression, of the Earth.

You might ask, then, how does it manifest that we know of other realms, non-physical, wherein limitation exists? Now you have found a key of empowerment, of wisdom. It is this mechanism that perpetuates karma (remembering karma to be the opportunity, neither good nor bad). Actually, karma is lovingly neutral. The entity who bears the karma determines its direction, positive or negative. See?

So, look you here… An entity twenty lifetimes past has carried a remorse with them when passing through the veil separating the Earth from other realms of expression… the doorway, the portal you call death. They carry this to another place, another consciousness. Because it is limiting, they cannot carry it to, let us say, the next major realm of expression, which is light-filled, for it cannot exist there, not in that form. So they must go to a realm of familiarity, a sort of symbiotic relationship where entities of like mind can dwell and experience their common limitation. In this case, let us say the entity has remorse for a misdeed of his or her own action. They come back to the Earth when it is appropriate, carrying the seeds of this remorse, and might do so for twenty lifetimes.

And now, in this, the twenty-first, the seeds bear fruit, because the (quote) "soil of the Earth" (end quote) is appropriate to nourish those seeds once again. Perhaps the same entities who were transgressed against, that predicated the remorse of this soul, are here again. So all the entities involved are presented with an opportunity to release these limitations. For this entity is the perpetrator and has remorse, and the others might be the victims or the recipients of some misdeed, and perhaps they hold anger or even hatred, and they know not why. This powerful key then enables you to not only free that one who has come before thee seeking, but to free many.

When the Disciples could not heal this one, it was because of the power, the long-standing presence of the karmic interaction of these devils – or dis-ease, or limitations – and the proximity of those who were connected to that karma.

Now, you will see why the Master oft-times said, *Do not return to the village. Do not pass through the town in which you live, but go around it,* because those who are the fragments of the past are dwelling therein; those who carry the power of the perpetuation of the thought-form of limitation, and thus disease, live in the village. And the healing is complete when it has been fully accepted.

COMPLETE VERSUS INCOMPLETE HEALINGS

Notice this, for it's an important point, one which many, if not all of you, will encounter here and there, if you choose to walk the path of life and do the Father's good healing works...

One Who Has Faith, But Residual Karma

An entity can come before you and ask, "Oh, dear Lord _____... " (and you can insert your own name here, please) "I know thou to be the daughter of God/the son of God. If thou would but say the word, I know that I am healed." And so you look at them and you see within, you feel, you know, you can sense, perhaps you feel with your body, perhaps you see with your physical eyes, perhaps you have visions, insights, a collage of past lives. And you know immediately that you can answer this call. But you also know that the entity probably will not fully manifest the healing.

Why would you do it? Because you know that the path is open for the entity, and that a wondrous work, interconnected with other souls who have karma here, can be made manifest. So you say unto the entity, "Do you believe?" And they answer, "Yea, I believe thou art the daughter of God/the son of God, that God's Light shines through thee in word and touch. I beseech thee, heal thou me." And yet, you see the spirit of that one standing apart from these words, not departing but apart. And you see that in this distance between the consciousness of this entity and the spiritual acceptance within them, there are yet shadows. Yet, it is asked of thee, and thus thou give it. The entity might in that moment burst into light and manifest a healing and run about proclaiming their healing, and perhaps hours later, or a day or two, it has faded.

This can bring a powerful remorse. It can bring to the surface of that entity's consciousness the recognition that there is yet some facet within that hasn't claimed their worthiness to be healed. For as you are asking them "Do you believe," the addendum to that is, "that thou art worthy of forgiveness? Do you believe that you are worthy of receiving God's grace? Do you believe that in answering the above, that you can now let God's grace pass through you to the others?" See the wisdom here? You have known there are others involved. In order for this entity's healing to be fruitful, they must be not only willing to receive healing grace themselves, but to allow this healing grace to flow all through them and to those against whom they have held some thought, some shadow of limitation.

We pray that we are giving this to you in ways which are understandable. It is so very beautifully simple and pure, and it is our prayer that these words will help to empower you. If an entity, such as in this example, comes back in a day or two or a lunar cycle and has some form of emotion, perhaps they are frustrated, they might even be angry with you, or aggressive, or challenge you, "Art thou truly the daughter of God? If so, why am I not healed?" What is this, if not the shadowy Forces attempting to take away your righteousness? Remember, they know of your presence wherever you are in the Earth. Mass-mind thought is of one consciousness, just as God's Spirit is of omnipotent consciousness.

The Wonder and Opportunity of Contrast

We've explained why the Spirit of God does not vanquish shadows or darkness, but let us briefly re-state that here. You see the beauty of a gem when the master gem-cutter cleaves it only after careful study, evaluation, consideration, thought, perhaps even meditation and prayer; they look for the lines of cleavage that will most bring out the beauty of the gem within; they envision the finished gem within the rough stone and cleave it accordingly.

Once this is done, the facets, the planes of cleavage, use light and darkness to bring forth brilliance, to manifest the color, to augment and to facilitate the light. Again, how can one truly know light without the presence and beauty of darkness to contrast it?

Darkness is not evil. It is the thought of those who would dwell in it, seeking to elude what they perceive as the Light of God by so doing. And yet, all is of God.

So when the entity returns to you and chastises you or is bitter or perhaps lamenting (any variant is possible here; these entities are highly creative, with a note of loving humor), look for that center of light, that place of joyful peace. Claim your own laughter, your own love, your righteousness, your authority. And state, "Get thee behind me, O limitation, for I am the messenger of God's Light. If ye seek it in truth, then open self. Do you believe that you are worthy of God's grace? Do you believe that the others against whom you hold judgment are also worthy?"

They may burst into tears. They may stomp away in anger, because they cannot. But if they remain, they are likely ready. The Master knew these things, and still knows them, and will work with you and through you to help you know them. See?

Thwarting Temptation

So, as the Master saw that the first healing (to use colloquial terms) broke through the first several layers of habit, of familiarity, and found some place of residency to grow and manifest within the dis-eased entity, He touched his eyes again and stated with authority, "Be thou healed. Go home, but do not go into the village," knowing that this second healing spoke to the last vestiges, the karmic fibrils of light, whose root lived in the village. And knowing the dis-eased entity to be in a very open, vulnerable, fresh, new state, He admonished him, "Go thou not back into temptation, lest this healing not endure because thy faith has not grown to match it."

THE NATURE OF HEALING

When you offer healing to an entity, you are offering them the calling forth of their own spiritual light. The Master did not call the woman a dog, but spoke of the low, subservient level of consciousness that she was dwelling in.

Calling Forth Another's Light

Notice this, the canine reference here is one of subservience, the submission of one's will to another external authority. And until this woman saw this, knew it, and empowered herself to come forth and claim freedom from it, the Master ignored her, looked the other way. Talk is cheap; action requires some effort. By ignoring the woman and trusting (with a note of loving humor) the Disciples, He did several things. He showed to them a quality within them that needed a bit of tidying up, some housecleaning, if you will.

One who has claimed righteousness and is living in a state of joyful ease, holding loving laughter, loving neutrality, within them, how could they become frustrated? How could they become angry? For they would see this woman as a child of God who is struggling to find the way out of the shadows of habit. And they would be enabled, because of their own claiming, to do as the Master: to look, to cast no judgment (to have a rather blank but passively joyful countenance), to offer nothing to the woman that could be... What? What would you think?

Not Fueling the Shadowy Force

Here is another key, a most valuable one: The Master's loving passivity, His seeming lack of interest, gave the woman's shadowy Forces of habit nothing to focus upon.

A fire cannot burn without fuel, can it? The flame of habit, limitation, shadow or darkness, needs the fuel of opposition, resistance, in order to perpetuate itself. Darkness cannot endure without a source of nutritive. It is parasitic in nature, and yet can be transformed to be benevolent... so very simple. Had the Master resisted when this woman was submissive to the forces of habit... As a dog submits to its master who might literally be beating it, so was this woman.

Sons and Daughters of the Law of One

"I am come to bring bread to the children of Israel." Is this a place? Is this a city? A village? No. The children of Israel are the Sons and Daughters of God. They are not a certain religion, a certain faith, a certain creed or dogma. Those are things of mankind's doing, not God's. The children of Israel are the Sons and Daughters of the Law of One, still incarnating into the Earth, joyfully experimenting, playfully challenging themselves and God's Laws so that they might the better understand. For their ultimate goal or destination is to become co-creators with God. It brings God great joy that we so do.

God does not lament our inequities, but He knows and sees them to be the purification process, that which brings enlightenment. He knows the darkness to be of her own creation, his own creation.

THESE TIMES

Now, dear friends, you are in those cycles in the Earth where these Forces may well unite. But you are the channels of blessing. Yours is the opportunity to manifest, to make the way passable, to open yourselves and inspire others, to claim forgiveness for self that you can make it possible for those with whom you are connected to accept forgiveness, as well.

Opening the Way for Self and Others

Imagine being connected to dozens, hundreds, thousands of other souls (some more brilliantly than others). And that, let us say, a great number of these connective lines of light from the past, from the future, from the present, are dulled because of limiting thought or emotion, and that forgiveness is the key or vessel which can cleanse these and enable the light to flow. How much more brilliant could you be, were you to so do?

The Law of Just Return

So, then, look at the entity who comes before you, and ask self, "If I answer this call and impart God's grace as His channel of blessing, am I not also imparting that grace to myself?" For, thousands of connections of intersecting lines away, there might be one who has a direct line of light to you today, who will benefit and pass that light back to you. How manifold over? Multiplied by the number of entities who are served. So another Law is revealed to you, hopefully in some clarity.

The Power of Belief

You can take spittle and the dust of the earth and combine them, and place them over the eyes of one who cannot see, and necessarily so, because thou hast done it in God's Name, it becomes holy. The power of the Master is not something unattainable. You already have it. If you could reach down and grasp several pinched tufts of dust from the earth and place your spittle into it, swirl it around, and empower it with your faith, it would be healing. It would have healing properties.

The Law of Expectancy

Belief is the power behind healing. You must have such a belief that there is no question that you are a channel of blessings to those who come to you. You cannot attach yourself to the outcome. For if you do, you impose the Law of Expectancy, and that expectancy is resident in the Earth, isn't it? Therefore, you've come full cycle and brought your own healing potential back into the throes of the shadows.

The Thought Is What Makes It So

Now, to make a distinction here once again: The Shadows are lovingly neutral, the Light is lovingly neutral. Together, the beauty is remarkable, incomprehensible. It is the thought that is placed into same, either, in any such realm, that is empowering.

CLOSING COMMENTS

A prayer: The Path of the Christ:

O Great Spirit of God, Thou art my Mother, my Father. I am one with Thee. In this realm in which I am now focused, I empower myself, because I know myself to be of Thee. Help Thou me to see all things as a part of Thy Spirit. So doing, I claim my authority to be in command of all that comes before me. I claim Thy Law. I claim Thy presence in my word and action. All these I do in the name of my Brother, the Master, the Christ, affirming His presence with me always. Amen.

See? In this manner.

We are through here for the present. But know we are with thee, as well. If thou would ask it in God's name, we as His Children, as well, shall joyfully answer and walk with you.

You are never alone. Know this, claim it, and our power becomes a living testimony of light to the wonder and glory of God's Spirit.

13 - *Jesus and the Fisherman*

LAMA SING COMMENTARY

It came to pass that the Master was seated by the seashore beneath a small but graceful tree, whose branches arched out, providing shelter and shade to Him and those of His Disciples with Him.

A short distance away, near the seashore, are another grouping of individuals, among whom we find Tal and Eno, two fishermen contemplating the sea and the sky beyond. Others of their grouping, also fishermen, have stated firmly they shall not go forth this day, for on the horizon are the indicators of a forthcoming storm. Yet Eno and Tal, pacing back and forth contemplating the rush on the surface of the water just barely visible on the horizon, knowing that a great school of fish are therein, they make their decision, and mount their craft. It has a small mast and equally small sail, and two sets of oars. To the stern is a mound of net.

As they begin to laboriously pull upon their sets of oars, several of the others call out to them, "Come back. It is not wise. It is, indeed, dangerous to go forth this day."

From His position somewhat above and beyond this grouping, the Master can see them. His eyes focus on them, as they pull mightily upon their oars, and their craft responds, cutting through the waters, which are, in the moment, quite calm. As He continues to gaze upon them, He does not hesitate in His speech or comment in answer to the questions being presented to Him by those who are with Him.

"The meaning of Truth," the Master continues softly, "is held in the hearts and minds of those who perceive it."

"What about the truths that are written," Stephen asks softly, "and those which are held as the rod against which all is measured by the priests and lawgivers and such? Should we perceive Truth as you say it, O Lord, and find it divergent to that which is upheld, how are we to act?"

Glancing at Stephen, the Master turns again to look upon the horizon, the craft of Tal and Eno becoming more and more diminished as they move steadily, pursuing the great school of fish they seek. "The Truth within you," the Master responds softly, "is likened unto a temple of light. It is such that all things can be seen, if thou would take whatsoever is your quest, your need, into this temple of Truth within you. Therein, it shall be seen according to the Will of God and according to that which is never by the interpretation of one or more outwardly. For theirs is conditioned by that which they hold as their quest, as their need, or as that which had brought them to their current point of being. But the temple of Truth within you shines clearly, with honor and truth for all things."

Turning to look at Stephen, the Master smiles, "It is good to honor that which has honor, but never to the diminishment of the Truth you find in the temple within you. That Truth, above all else, is the Light which will guide you steadily, honorably, and safely to your journey's end."

"And if there is conflict between my inner Truth and their truth, how am I to act, O Lord?"

"Give honor to that which calls upon you for honor," the Master responds, "but never to the comprise of the Truth within you. Ever hear that call, and answer it."

Excitedly, they are dropping their net, and have raised their small sail to aid them in trying to encircle the great school of fishes. Their focus is so intent upon their quest that Tal and Eno notice not that the sky has darkened and that great swirling clouds are rolling towards them and towards the shoreline, now almost beyond their sight. The roar of thunder and the pounding waves of rain strike them without warning, and they begin to scurry back and forth across their small craft.

"What are we to do with the fishes?" Eno questions of Tal.

"They are so great, but look you, the waves are growing," and their vessel is now bobbing to and fro wildly.

"We will release all but a few, enough for our sustenance," and so they do.

The wind has torn the sail from two of its mooring places, and it flaps angrily in the wind. They take it down and seat themselves, and begin to pull on their oars, striving mightily to keep the bow of their vessel toward the oncoming waves.

Again and again the waves crash over them, and yet they pull and toil. The moments merge into hours, and the hours seem to be as days, or longer. The darkness is all about, and the wind spins their vessel in spite of their greatest labors. All through the night and into the morn, yet dark, do they toil. And the sea rages. They are exhausted, and though it is day, it is likened unto night, for the dark, swirling, ominous clouds let none of the sun's rays through.

Subsiding somewhat, Tal glances about the sea, and as Eno is scooping up the water from their vessel and pouring it out over the side, Tal begins to secure the oars. Eno lets down a bit of the net to keep the vessel in alignment, so to say, and they look about, seeing naught.

Tal comments, "I feel we are lost. Come. Let us pray," and so they do.

The day passes, and night falls again, and still there is naught but darkness. Great swirling walls of mist descend upon them, indeed so thick, it is difficult for Tal to see Eno, his brother, at the other end of his small vessel.

"Rest now, my brother," Tal comments to Eno. "I will keep the watch."

Finding some comfort against the great bundle of netting behind him, swiftly Eno drifts off into sleep.

Seated at the forefront of the vessel, Tal, looking about and seeing naught but the mist, bows his head. "Lord God? It is I, Tal. I come before Thee, humbly asking on behalf of my brother, Eno, that Thou would spare him. For his life is yet young in its journey, and there is much I know that Thou have prepared for him as gifts. Forgive me that I have taken him into this great peril. I ask only that You deliver him unto safety, and if it is Thy Will, I gladly come to Thee if Thou would grant but this prayer. O Lord, let me hear Thee. Let me know Thou art, even now, with us."

The Master sits up sharply, and several of the other Disciples note this quickly. He rises to His feet and a number of the Disciples do the same. Others remain deep in sleep.

Looking down at the seashore, the Master turns and removes from a branch of the tree a beautiful set of wind chimes, given as a gift of love to Him by one of the villagers to whom He gave His grace some days ago. Carefully removing it from the branch, the Master strides swiftly down to the seashore's edge. There is the captain of a small vessel, which is moored just a distance off shore. "I would that you would take me to sea," the Master comments softly, His eyes aglow.

"At this hour?" the captain questions. "We can see naught, and look you, my Lord," for he knoweth of the Master, "one can see but only a short distance."

"If you would," the Master questions softly, His eyes filled with love, "take me to sea. It is God that calls, not I of myself."

Looking at the wind chimes curiously, held in the Master's hand, and then into the Master's eyes, the captain states, "You have only but to speak the word. I know of thee, and I shall answer. Come!" and he calls to his seamen. They board a small vessel, along with the Master and two of the Disciples, and they row to the small sailing vessel moored a distance away. Soon they are at sea.

The captain, walking about, turns to look at the Master, who is seated on a small perch towards the bow of the ship. "Good Lord," the captain asks softly, smiling, "what is the intention you have for those wind chimes?"

Smiling, the Master extends them forth to the captain. "I would that you would place them there," pointing to the pole of a sort that juts forth from the bow of the vessel, "that it might be known, perhaps, as the voice of God singing out, guiding us in our journey."

The captain rubs the side of his face, and you can hear the raspy sound of his bewhiskered cheek as he does. He laughs softly. "Never have I had such a request of me, Lord," and he turns and gestures to one of his seamen, telling him to move out on the spinnaker pole and fasten this on the outer point, where there is a loop to so do.

The seaman, eyebrows arched, questions not the captain, but ponders within, to what end? Carefully, he makes his way to the end of the great pole, thrust forth from the bow of this vessel, and secures the wind chimes to its point. Then, sliding back carefully, he steps off behind the Master and the captain, who are now seated just a few steps away from the bow of the vessel. The Master smiles and nods, as the tinkling sound of the wind chimes fills the air, seemingly echoing off the heavy mist that surrounds the vessel.

"What is my course, my Lord?"

"Where the Will of God takes us," the Master answers, smiling, gesturing straightaway with His hand, pointing to the forefront.

"What hast thou heard," questions Stephen.

"Yes," adds James, "what is it that inspires us on this journey?" James continues, laughing softly, "I think you could agree with me, Lord, this is curious."

The Master turns and smiles, and laughs gently with both of them. "It is to answer the call that I have heard within."

"In dream?" Stephen asks.

"What is, truly, a dream?" the Master answers. "That which one believes? Or that which one thinks is only illusion? And how does one differentiate?" he asks. "Is slumber the doorway through which one passes from reality into illusion? Or could it be possible," and the Master laughs gently again, "that the reverse is true… that the illusion is here," tapping on the top of the cabin rail that He is perched on, "and that truth and reality lie beyond..." now tapping His forefinger on His heart, "...here. That we enter this, the Kingdom of God and the Truth of God, through the portal called sleep?"

James is shaking his head to and fro, smiling. "Ah, Lord. Your words have such meaning for me. But when I attempt to apply them, as you speak these words, they are not quite the same," and he laughs again.

"Nor I," Stephen answers. "It is as though I know your words are of truth, but when I strive to truly live them, something happens and they are not as powerful as when you speak them."

With a generous smile, and love in the gaze with which He bathes Stephen and James, the Master allows some time for them to hear their own words, and feel them. And then we hear, "The purpose of the journey is to know the Truth of who and what you are in the eternal sense. What you experience here," again tapping the substance of wood upon which He is perched, "and what you experience here," again tapping His heart, "are actually no different. It is how you, James, perceive them, and what you decide to do with that perception that opens the way, and makes it passable.

"And you, Stephen, you view from the gaiety of one who believes in Truth – my Truth, as I give it unto thee from our God – that you see not the wellspring within you, that is one and the same as with mine."

Smiling greatly, Stephen answers, "Ah, these words you have given unto me oft in past, Lord. Do know this... I hear them, and I am seeking this. Before this journey's end, I promise you, I shall know that wellspring, and I shall ever find you at the edge of it. Always."

The Master cups His chin in His hand, studying Stephen, and then James. Then He smiles, tilts His head back and laughs a gentle but gay laugh. "The strength with which thy spirit calls unto thee is evident to me. You, my brothers, dear unto my heart, ever shall I seek you at that wellspring of Truth within you. And Stephen? I am of no doubt that we shall oft be together, as you have said, at the holy place within you."

His breathing is labored, and his body aches with the pain of the laborious effort they have put forth to keep their vessel aright. The thought fades in and out of Tal's mind and consciousness, as the wind might carry a fragrance of spring flowers down a hillside to a villager seated comfortably, securely, on a bench before his abode.

But this is not a bench. Nor is Tal in comfort before his abode, but seated upon the bow of his tiny vessel, in the midst of a great sea, surrounded with a wall of mist, lost. "If only You would speak to me, Lord, that as I feel my life moving, like the currents of this great sea, to some unknown destination, I am willing. If it is Thy Will, I come unto Thee. Joyful. But, speak Thou to me, if You would." His head pounds, and fingers of throbbing pain are thrust into his body here and there. He sighs deeply, and slumps back to rest his head upon the gunnel, his eyes looking up at the mist, somewhat luminous now, above him.

And then he hears it. At first he thinks it is but a dream, something that comes to him out of pain and fatigue. And then he hears it again, a bit more boldly, tinkling, jingling. He pulls himself upright with the last of his strength, and there is silence. And then, again, a delicate, tinkling.

"Eno!" he calls. "Eno!"

Eno stirs, rubbing himself. His arms and legs ache so badly, it is difficult for him to get them moving. He bends his head upward, and can barely make out his brother's form at the bow of the vessel, only a few feet away.

"Yes, my brother! What is it?" looking about with anticipation. His heart sinks. There is nothing but the mist.

"Listen! Listen, my brother," Tal calls out.

Straining, Eno listens. "I hear nothing."

"Listen. Be still. Listen."

And then he hears it. A gentle tinkling sound, barely audible, but clear, as though the mist itself is conducting the sound, amplifying it, carrying it to them. "What can that be?" Eno calls out, pulling himself erect, now very attentive. "We are at sea. How can we hear such a sound? It is the Spirit-call chimes, those they use in some of the temples."

The Master rises, and steps to the very bow of the vessel, glancing for a moment at the wind chimes perched at the very end of the pole.

Listening carefully, He turns and calls out to the captain, gesturing. "If you would, please, direct the vessel, but slowly, if you will, in this direction."

The captain is puzzled, but questions Him not, and calls out the order. One sail comes down, and only another powers the vessel, slowly, through the water.

The Master, peering off into the mist, begins to smile. He turns back to Stephen and James, and states, "You see? As one heeds the call within, there is, at the end of such a journey, a good purpose, a joyful service. But one must trust in the Truth of that inner temple."

They look at one another, still puzzled, for they have not heard the call of Eno and Tal as yet.

"To what end, Lord?" Stephen questions. "What are we doing? What is this about?"

The Master raises His hand and waves about to call for silence, then cups a hand to His ear, motioning Stephen and James to come to the forefront where He stands, and to listen.

Their faces are blank at first, but James is the first to hear. His mouth comes open. His eyebrows arch, and then he smiles and nods to the Master, who has stepped back, leaning against the vessel rail just a step away from them, watching. "I hear it, Lord! I hear it," and then Stephen, as well.

The Master nods at James, and James scurries down to the captain's position and directs him, pointing off into the mist, and then holding his hand to his ear, indicating that the captain might do the same. Suddenly the captain's face lights up, and he issues orders loudly.

Stephen leans over the bow, calling out, "Hell-o-o-o!"

Tal's head is bowed. A tear falls from one eye, and lands upon the seat just by his feet. "What a sweet answer, Lord, in the beautiful simplistic sound of those sacred chimes. I know not who comes forth to answer my prayer, but if Thou would, I offer myself in service to You. From this day onward, whatsoe'er is mine to give, I give it from the joy of mine heart. Bring that to me that which Thou would and guide Thou me, that I shall know the way and the works Thou would have me do. I am thine evermore."

He places His arms, one upon each shoulder, of Stephen and James as they lean upon the vessel railing to peer into the mist, which is now beginning to fade.

They can see the tiny vessel bobbing on the sea ahead, and as Stephen and James each reciprocate by placing an arm around the Master, as well, the Master is smiling and nodding, His eyes fixed upon the vessel.

"Ah-h, my brothers, God has sent us a brother, one who will join us in these works, and who will carry the Light of God's truth forward unto others who are, as they have been, lost, upon the sea of life."

14 - The Transfiguration of Jesus

CHANNEL/AL MINER: This is a request for a topical research reading titled The Transfiguration of Jesus. I'm going to read from the Bible, Matthew 17, verses 1 through 13.

And after six days Jesus taketh Peter, James, and John his brother, and bringeth them up into an high mountain apart,

And was transfigured before them: and his face did shine as the sun, and his raiment was white as the light.

And, behold, there appeared unto them Moses and Elias talking with him.

Then answered Peter, and said unto Jesus, Lord, it is good for us to be here: if thou wilt, let us make here three tabernacles; one for thee, and one for Moses, and one for Elias.

While he yet spake, behold, a bright cloud overshadowed them: and behold a voice out of the cloud, which said, This is my beloved Son in whom I am well pleased; hear ye him.

And when the disciples heard it, they fell on their face, and were sore afraid.

And Jesus came and touched them, and said, Arise, and be not afraid.

And when they had lifted up their eyes, they saw no man, save Jesus only.

And as they came down from the mountain, Jesus charged them, saying, Tell the vision to no man, until the son of man be risen again from the dead.

And his disciples asked him, saying, Why then say the scribes that Elias must first come?

And Jesus answered and said unto them, Elias truly shall first come, and restore all things.

But I say unto you, That Elias is come already, and they knew him not, but have done unto him whatsoever they listed. Likewise shall also the son of man suffer of them. **Then the disciples understood that he spake unto them of John the Baptist.**

SPONSOR'S QUESTION

The transfiguration of Jesus seems to be a major event in His life. Would you please discuss what it meant in the life of Jesus and what it means in our own lives?

LAMA SING COMMENTARY

Perceive then, dear friends, what has been spoken in that given above. Envision what has gone before. The efforts, the journeys, the encounters, and that these three are chosen to traverse with the Master unto a certain height, thereupon finding the revelation that the kingdom of the Father has entered into the Earth in the fullness of its beauty and its hope and promise for all those whom were willing.

THE UNIFICATION

Here we find the symbolic to be clear, for as the three chosen clearly symbolize, if not depict, the physical, the mental, and the spiritual. To an extent, there is the bringing of these three essentially separate expressions of the being unto the highest point of consciousness that can be obtained. Thereupon, to recognize the unification and to be unified into a state of joyous service and, through the unification, to be given those teachings and that power which is present through the knowledge of the Law: the affirmation and conformation of this spiritual bond to the expression of spirituality embodied in man.

Revealing the Light

So, symbolically, there is, in these writings and in the occurrence itself, the unification which occurs in each soul at that time when the soul has prepared itself and is willing to receive same. That it can divest from its consciousness those things which previously were as the limitation, or as that which may appear as a cloak around a light of some brilliance. To wit then, as such a cloak may be removed, the light then must become apparent to all who can see.

The importance here is also present in the choice of the Disciples to journey with Him. These then, each one, were given a certain gift befitting their consciousness, and each one was given some additional opportunity to go beyond their own sense of limitation of their expression.

Applies to All

And so do we find that within this as yet given, the symbology, the same applies to each of thee, dear friends. Each of thee having, in essence, the composition as depicted in the Disciples, and each, perhaps, summarily being found as given: Peter, James, and John.

When thee in thy efforts in Earth or in any realm make such an effort so as to rise to that point of consciousness as to receive from God His blessing, then it becomes the bringing together of these Forces: an end to the separateness, a joyous unification into one consciousness of the multiple expressions of self.

It is at this time or through this activity that ye will find the enjoinment of all such previous forces unto thy work and unto thy purpose. For then this affirmation becomes a unifying of self in terms of the will as an individual with that of the Will Universal and Eternal of God. So we can find here throughout this particular teaching the encouragement for each of thee to go forth and to seek this unifying of mind, body, and spirit.

Transference of the Gift

In the journey there was the discourse which brought forth the uniqueness of the individuals. In the presence of the transformation, the illumination, and the heightening of energies in and about the Lord Jesus, there was the transference of these forces unto each of the Disciples present. So that each would henceforth carry an aspect, a portion, of this unto the lands of their brethren, and so that they, as sowers of good seed, would be present to answer those calls as would so benefit from that which they had to give.

Of course, the occurrences which followed were such so as to complete this for them. But for each of thee, the teaching in this, the transformation, is profound to each level of your expression. As thee reflect or meditate upon this, consider this from the three aspects of your consciousness.

SYMBOLS OF THE UNIFICATION

Consider how such would feel in the physical... Here, One you respect and follow becomes as the Light itself.

Total Radiation of Light

And in the Light there comes an emanation, which penetrates fairly through unto thy core, or soul. And there comes the appearance of those who are recognized for their oneness with God and His work. And so then, find, as ye will receive the Light, there comes into each of thee the wisdom, the spirit and teaching, and the manifestation of this into the oneness of the personage: the man Jesus.

And so then, returning to this, in essence, as a teaching, consider then that the Master came unto the Light as though He were the Light, that the Light radiated from every aspect of His being. It did not radiate from just a hand, a finger, or in just this certain way or that. There was and is, clearly, the total envelopment and the total radiation of this Light at all levels. Conceive of one's face being as the sun itself. This is as to say that it could not be beheld with the eye, that it must be perceived with the consciousness beyond this, and that His raiment or garments did so emit the Light as pure and as powerful as can be conceived. Then this shows that the works of man, when in accordance with the Will of God, are as at one with God, and that His presence is without limitation, even though within the finite, as of the physical of mankind.

The Force Eternal

But what of the man Jesus at this moment?

There was the passage of that Force eternal into the centers of the being, the body; the alignment of these through the cumulative effort of incarnations past, and through the purification in the earlier days through the training and guidance of the great teachers; and then unto this moment wherein the Force eternal did, in effect, place an energy within this body such as might not be conceivable to the consciousness of a finite mind or an expressed physical form. So this, then, in terms of a stimulating energy, did awaken each of these and bring them to their fullest. Wherein the vibration of all the major centers was such so as to make for even the garments, the ground, the ethers, and all that surrounded the Master, to vibrate purely and fully simply through His presence.

Moses: The Holder of Universal Law

Then there is the presence of Moses, who is the Lawgiver, who holds the tenets to the Law Universal, who then giveth unto his children, his peoples, the Word of God, whom is the bearer of the Word. So the Word is given as a gift through the vibration or presence of Moses.

Elias: The Holder of the Staff of Righteousness

And then cometh unto the Master His companion of the earlier years, His friend, and His supporter, and we find that in Elias there was given the tools, the gift of workmanship. In effect, the Staff of Righteousness was given, and the anointment completed through the love and admiration of this soul, who was also called John the Baptist.

And the bonding of their spiritual love for one another and the presence of the Spirit of God unified the soul of man into harmony at a certain cycle within the spheres. (Some call this a certain cycle of the spheres denoted approximately every two thousand one hundred eighty Earth years. But this is not of major import in what is being given here. It is given for a reference point.)

MEANING FOR ALL

In the presence, then, of these well-loved souls, one with the other, there is the final purification and preparation unto the Forces of all realms, unto the will of the body, and unto the spiritual Force, which cometh unto a bearer of the Word and Works of the Father.

Reach Beyond

This means unto each of thee, that, so as thee create for self a willingness, a desire, to reach beyond self in terms of what you see, what you feel, and how you relate to the forces of Earth, then this maketh the path open for the Law, which is as the Word, and the mantle or staff, and anointment, which is the recognition of thy presence and thy oneness or bond with God's Will. So we find that these as tools can become of such beauty so as to remove all limitation and all potentiality for doubt or fear to obstruct that flow of pure light through thee.

A Defining Moment for Jesus

In terms of the progression of the man called Jesus, this was, indeed, a point of major demarcation. It is as though (in our humble viewing) the Master traveled through the entirety of the life to this point: to receive these gifts and this blessing. For, from henceforth, His true ministry and fulfillment of the prophecy would enter its final stages.

Pivotal Gift for All

As heard then, the voice, or the Word, of God at this moment, there is the fear among the Disciples in several aspects. Firstly, was the fear of the loss of the individuality, the concern for the ill preparedness of their being, and many other such aspects which flow instantaneously through their consciousness. It is only after the Master's own touch and comforting bring them into a rebalanced state that they begin to realize or be cognizant of what has transpired there upon the mount. Then each of them, in their own manner, began their reflection.

Opportunities to Evolve

Peter, of course, as was his nature (with a note of loving humor, and yet is) questioned openly, lovingly, and without the pretense or reservation that could be found among certain of the others. Of his questions did he, then, find guidance for his own soul, perhaps one of the most beautiful and one of the most powerful that can be easily found in the holy writings: the evidence of man's promise to have not one opportunity but many; that, so as Elias was present did he come again as John the Baptist, just so do each of thee have the opportunity to evolve yourselves, to evolve your consciousness, through such experiences as thee might choose in accordance with thy need.

Opportunities to Serve

And unto those who had been enangered of the Master previously because He did not aid John, there came in the moment of understanding that this was the fulfillment of the prophecy: that even so as the Master knew of it, so then did John know of it and did become a joyous servant in accordance with it, the Word.

Opportunities to Know Our Divine Nature

For even so as unto your present times, dear friend, is the Word among you. And even so unto your times is the Word given again and again, humbly but with joyous hope and with the anticipation that through the expression of said Word there would come about the ultimate realization within each soul, each entity in the Earth, their eternal and divine nature.

THE GIFT

But returning unto the experience upon the mountain, clearly the Master stated His willingness to allow the will of man its due, to give unto man that which he would claim and that which he would seek as his will. Even here, this entity, who only moments ago clearly was the embodiment of the Spirit of God, causing the vibrations and energies to fair illuminate beyond description all that was about, now with humbleness and almost meekness stated that He was willing to submit to the will of man.

What manner of being could knowingly walk while yet in a physical body unto such a future? Is there among you one who would knowingly endure such? Yes, you are willing. It is you unto who we speak at this moment. Thou art truly willing, for as the Master walked, He walked not alone.

Oneness for All Time

And as His body was borne through the Earth by His will, the will of many others was known unto Him, for He did see with eternal sight, and their presence and their strength was His to command. There was never that time wherein He dwelled alone, for this bond formed upon the mountain also aligned the Forces of Light into a state of glorious oneness that shall endure throughout eternity. It is as though there were previously legions of light – each unto their own works, unique – and at this moment, drawn together by the Will of God who they did each seek to serve with the fiber of their being. And as the Light bound them and these legions unto oneness of purpose, henceforth evermore shall they joyously serve as a beautiful chord in the realms of eternity.

Transferring the Gift to All

What does this, then, mean unto you? It means that these aspects within you have also been united. It is this, then, which gives thee the meat of thy spiritual life. It is this, then, which gives thee the continuity of the search, the fulfillment, and the reward, if you will, of each day's service. It may, unto some aspects of reason in the Earth, be curious as to how such an occurrence of beauty could be relegated to a simple discovery of a statement, or of a validation, on the part of the Master of that called reincarnation.

The Promise of Eternity

But what a beautiful gift to give to these entities, that they might spread unto others — to know that the hope of tomorrow is an eternal hope. Witness, then, there is such power in this occurrence, that it even survived the purging of the Holy Writings and the councils and judgments which sought to make it unto their own will. So then, does it make its way known into your hearts and minds, that ye might not be so bound with fervor for this or that in the current incarnation, because thou art freed by the promise of eternity to know self and to know God. It is as to state: place no great judgment against thyself, but have faith and joy in the promise of those opportunities yet to come.

DO THESE THINGS

We would pray that each of thee can find in that which is given in the Holy Writing, and as well that given above, a stimulation to thy spiritual strength which will be sufficient to carry thee forth unto thine own mountain.

Elevate Self

As this might be apart from other mounts, it is apart from other aspects of yourself: a point of high accomplishment, symbolized by the mountain; it is also a literal depiction, in that thee must rise above the aspects of the Earth (in many aspects, literally) in order that thee can find those forces of energy or vibration which can be perceived with greater ease due to the lack of conflicting energies which might otherwise cloud these from thy perception.

This is not so as to say that there are not among thee such as can perceive the presence of this Force, this being of God wheresoe'er thou dwell, and that, to be sure, there are certain among thee who can find this oneness with God in all manner of place. But remember... a mount is a projection which elevates. And so the symbolic, and as well the literal, can be considered here, that thee must elevate above that which is common or preponderant in life.

Make Peace to Prepare the Way

It is the nature, further, of this teaching to give unto you another certain truth… Whereupon Peter in his, indeed, innocent boldness (for which he is endeared by so many) did be in askance of the Master, "Howbeit, O Lord, that it is stated, 'First must come Elias'?" to which the Master responded, "Indeed, truly Elias must first come and restore all things," So there must come that which is a maker of peace, of harmony, that which prepares the way.

Recognize the Truth

So find in this that thee must put forth a certain effort in your own lives which makes the way perceptive, receptive, sensitive, and harmonious. This, then, is a force of will which recognizes, in a state of profound truth, each certain thing for what it truly is; and each entity – great or lesser, man or woman, king or pauper – for what is in their heart moreso than for what is upon their body or among their possessions. And that this loving truth should reach unto them, and invite or encourage, that they make aright in their own temple (which is as to say their own house, their own home, their own dwelling, within their body, mind, and spirit of consciousness) so as to be receptive for those forces which will follow, borne by the Lamb of God, the Master. So as this was affirmed, as the Master came unto John for the anointment, the baptism, it was to affirm unto John that his work was well done, and completed nearly to its fullness.

And so we find, then, that for each of thee, the way must be made clear. The peacemaker must come before that which will gain. The prophet of truth, and that which is of honor within each of thee, must be willing to recognize every aspect that comprises your consciousness.

Rejoice in the Presence of God

If, in this the teaching, we might find that one of the Disciples would, instead of entering into fear, have rejoiced, and, with upraised hands and arms, praised God for His presence, and placed their thanks and their affirmation at the foot of God then present within the body of the man Jesus, they may then have been complete. But it was, you see, not their time.

So find from this that, as ye rejoice in the discovery of each aspect within your own being, fear it not, the discovery. Fear not to see, to know, and to lovingly understand the nature of thy being. But with grace and with joyous compassion, know yourselves; and know from yourselves, then, thy brethren. For it is wisely written that each of ye are the mirrors into which one can see the eternal nature of thine own soul.

THE MASTER'S INVITATION

In this, then, we find the clear invitation from the Master that ye would seek this mountain, and that ye would seek to unify all of the expressions of your being into a oneness. That this, then, would be affirmed in a moment of return unto God, and that the result would be the affirmation dwelling with thee that the Word would be upon thee, that the power of the Word would be thine to use in His service, upon His work, and to His purpose.

What of these times in the Earth? There are many who speak of them with apprehension and with fear. There are certain who will, out of varying cause, dwell upon that which appears to be of detriment, vis-a-vis then, that of, as ye call the Earth Changes... the chaotic influence, the downfall of this or that. But if ye would take ear, and hear from that given above, and if ye would look unto these as just those things spoken of moments ago, can ye not see these to be aspects which, when accepted and purified, do become those step-stones of light unto thine own mount of unification with God? Can there not be seen, then, as a people, as a nation, as an expression of consciousness, that here is offered unto mankind the step-stones which have the potential of raising the entirety of consciousness upon the Earth.

If a worldly thing, then, be lost, is then not a portion of the bondage placed upon thee by this thing also lost? Is not a portion of self thusly freed? Once having known such freedom an entity can subsequently have all manner of possession and never be bound again. Or they may have no possessions and be of great wealth.

But until such has come unto thee and departed, just so as the speaker of Truth came unto the Earth and departed, there cannot be known the Master's own teachings through His presence, His departure, and His return.

And so as ye, then, look upon these changes in and about the Earth, rejoice in the light which is present among them, and know that the workers of peace walk among ye even now. And know that, within your being, His spirit is stirring. His joy and His promise are awakening within.

CLOSING COMMENTS

So, dear friends, as we prepare to conclude this humble gathering, whenever there is seen one who is struggling, pray that the Light, as ye have heard it told of, may surround them. Ask that, so as it is in accordance with their will and purpose, they be given all that is needed and that they be capable of seeing it.

Many of you have felt a great strength of late. This has been felt, in many respects, as shifts of emotional energy, as shifts of mental thought and attitude, but with a strange, almost haunting, yet wonderfully lifting force. Ye have, through this, felt movement, and in some, the movement has been apart from the previously followed pathways.

As ever, there is a sense of some sadness and loss when the familiar is released. But hear well this promise: for each thing that thou art willing to release in His name, He shall give unto thee ten-fold to replace it. And then as these ten ye give unto those who are met in your journey, He shall give unto thee an hundred to replace it. And so as ye continue to give and receive, ye shall find self to be the bearer of such a light and joy so as to be beyond that which these humble words might express to thee.

So then, know that ye can always know the source and the emanation of the Light, and let self be guided by it and let your gifts be joyously accepted in the knowledge that thou art, indeed, each one truly worthy of what is given thee.

As we conclude, we give this prayer in your names, dear friends:

Eternal Father-Mother-God,
guide us now in this day, in this time,
in this consciousness,
that we shall ever feel and live this lifetime
in accord with the teachings the Master, the Christ,
has given to us for eternity.
And let us ever remember and hold
the love and the warmth of His presence
in the forefront of our consciousness.
For this blessed opportunity and for these joys,
we are filled to exception with joy.
Amen.

–Lama Sing

About Lama Sing

More than thirty years ago, for our convenience, the one through whom this information flows accepted the name Lama Sing, though it was stated they, themselves, have no need for names or titles.

"We identify ourselves only as servants of God, dedicated to you, our brothers and sisters in the Earth." –Lama Sing

About This Channel

"Channel is that term given generally to those who enable themselves to be, as much as possible, open and passable in terms of information that can pass through them from the Universal Consciousness or other such which are not associated in the direct sense with their finite consciousness of the current incarnation." –Lama Sing

BOOKS BY AL MINER & LAMA SING

The Chosen: Backstory to the Essene Legacy
The Promise: Book I of The Essene Legacy
The Awakening: Book II of The Essene Legacy
The Path: Book III of The Essene Legacy

In Realms Beyond: Book I of The Peter Chronicles
In Realms Beyond: Study Guide
Awakening Hope: Book II of The Peter Chronicles
Return to Earth: Book III of The Peter Chronicle

Death, Dying, and Beyond: How to Prepare for The Journey Vol I
The Sea of Faces: How to Prepare for The Journey Vol II

Jesus: Book I
Jesus: Book II

The Course in Mastery

When Comes the Call

Seed Thoughts
Seed Thoughts to Consciousness

Stepstones: Compilation 1

The Children's Story

About Al Miner

A chance hypnosis session in 1973 began Al's tenure as the channel for Lama Sing. Since then, nearly 10,000 readings have been given in a trance state answering technical and personal questions on such topics as science, health and disease, history, geophysical, spiritual, philosophical, metaphysical, past and future times, and much more. The validity of the information has been substantiated and documented by research institutions and individuals, and those receiving personal readings continue to refer others to Al's work based on the accuracy and integrity of the information in their readings. In 1984, St. Johns University awarded Al an honorary doctoral degree in parapsychology.

Al conducts a variety of field research projects, as well as occasional workshops and lectures. He is no longer accepting requests for personal readings, but, rather, is devoting his remaining time to works intended to be good for all. Much of his current research is dedicated to the concept that the best of all guidance is that which comes from within. Al lives with his family in the mountains of Western North Carolina.

Made in the USA
Monee, IL
13 February 2025

12228078R00128